Company Taxation in the Asia-Pacific Region, India, and Russia

Dieter Endres • Clemens Fuest • Christoph Spengel
Editors

Company Taxation in the Asia-Pacific Region, India, and Russia

in collaboration with

Alexandra Bartholmeß, Christina Elschner,
Katharina Finke, Wei Li, Theresa Lohse,
Johannes Voget

Springer

Editors
Professor Dr. Dieter Endres
PricewaterhouseCoopers AG
Marie-Curie-Straße 24-28
60439 Frankfurt
dieter.endres@de.pwc.com

Professor Dr. Clemens Fuest
Said Business School
University of Oxford
Park End Street
Oxford OX1 1HP
United Kingdom
clemens.fuest@sbs.ox.ac.uk

Professor Dr. Christoph Spengel
University of Mannheim
Business School (BSUM)
Schloss, Ostflügel
68131 Mannheim
spengel@uni-mannheim.de

ISBN 978-3-642-12216-3 e-ISBN 978-3-642-12217-0
DOI 10.1007/978-3-642-12217-0
Springer Heidelberg Dordrecht London New York

Library of Congress Control Number: 2010927478

Cover design: WMXDesign GmbH, Heidelberg

Printed on acid-free paper

Springer is part of Springer Science+Business Media (www.springer.com)

Preface

This study provides an overview and extensive analysis of company taxation in the Asia-Pacific region, India, and Russia. It is not limited to a description of the taxation systems, but goes on to analyse the effective tax rates and their influence on foreign direct investment. For the first time the renowned methodology of Devereux/Griffith for determining effective tax rates has been applied to the Asia-Pacific region, India, and Russia in an international comparison. This methodology is now the standard approach to measuring effective tax burdens within the European Union.

The study has been prepared by a research consortium of PricewaterhouseCoopers, the Centre for European Economic Research (ZEW), the University of Mannheim, Germany, and the Oxford University Centre for Business Taxation (OUCBT), United Kingdom. The data on the corporate tax systems in the respective countries came from the local offices of PricewaterhouseCoopers; ZEW and the University of Mannheim were responsible for the description of the tax systems and for analysing the effective tax burden on companies; OUCBT undertook the empirical analysis.

We are grateful to all the numerous contributors to this study. Our special thanks go to Alexandra Bartholmess (PwC) who with great effort organized the data collection within the shortest possible time. We are indebted to the project team of ZEW, the University of Mannheim, and to OUCBT, namely to Christina Elschner, Katharina Finke, Theresa Lohse, Johannes Voget, and Wei Li without the support of whom we would not have been able to present such an extensive study.

Dieter Endres
PricewaterhouseCoopers, Frankfurt/Main

Clemens Fuest
Oxford University Centre for Business Taxation, Oxford

Christoph Spengel
University of Mannheim and ZEW, Mannheim

Contents

List of Figures

List of Tables

List of Abbrevation

AUD	Australian Dollar
BOI	Board of investment
CFC	Controlled foreign company
Chap.	Chapter
DB	Declining balance method
e.g.	Exempli gratia (for example)
EATR	Effective average tax rate
EMTR	Effective marginal tax rate
etc.	Et cetera
EU	European Union
FDI	Foreign direct investment
FIFO	First-in-first-out method
Fig.	Figure
FIPL	Foreign investment promotion law
FIZ	Foreign investment zone
GDP	Gross domestic product
HQ	Headquarters
i.e.	Id est (that is)
IDR	Indonesian Rupiah
IFS	The Institute of Fiscal Studies
INR	Indian Rupee
IPP	Investment priority plan
JPY	Japanese Yen
KRW	South Korean Won
LIFO	Last-in-first-out method
m	Million
MYR	Malaysian Ringgit
NHTE	New/High Technology Enterprise
No.	Number
OECD	Organization for Economic Co-operation and Development
OHQ	Operational headquarters

p.	Page
R&D	Research and development
ROH	Regional operations headquarters
SD	Sum of years' digits method
SEC	Section
SEZ	Special economic zone
SGD	Singapore Dollar
SL	Straight-line method
TWD	New Taiwan Dollar
ufd	Until fully depreciated
UNCTAD	United Nations Conference on Trade and Development
US	United States
USA	United States of America
var	Varying depreciation rate

Executive Summary

Objectives of the Study and the Model Applied (Chap. 1)

The Asia-Pacific region as well as India, and Russia have gained economic power among the world's economies and offer enormous sales opportunities for multinational companies. When considering a foreign direct investment in one of the countries of this region, the specific taxation framework constitutes one determinant to be accounted for in the decision making process of the multinational investor. Taking this into account, the objective of this study is threefold.

Firstly, the study provides a comparative analysis of the tax systems in thirteen territories of the Asia-Pacific region, namely Australia, Cambodia, China, Hong Kong, Indonesia, Japan, Malaysia, Philippines, Singapore, South Korea, Taiwan, Thailand, and Vietnam, plus India and Russia. The relevant information on the tax systems of these territories was collected in collaboration with Pricewaterhouse-Coopers and takes into account the tax law as of 1 January 2009 and amendments known to have entered into force during 2009.

Secondly, the study presents estimates of the effective levels of company tax burdens on domestic investments and cross-border investments in the Asia-Pacific region by multinationals located in either Germany or the United States. Effective tax burdens are relevant for investors' decisions on location, scale and mode of finance of a potential investment. The calculation of the effective tax levels is based on the approach of Devereux and Griffith (1999), which was also used by the European Commission carrying out comprehensive surveys on the comparison of effective tax burdens in the EU. Germany and the United States are considered as possible home countries of the multinational investor. Hence the analysis includes both, the perspective of a country applying the exemption method (Germany) and the perspective of a country applying the credit method (United States) to avoid the double taxation of foreign dividends.

In recent decades, governments across the world have become increasingly concerned about the impact of taxes on international investment flows. In Europe, the significant decline in corporate tax rates which occurred during the last two decades is widely seen as reflecting the forces of corporate tax competition. In East Asia, governments are at least as concerned about attracting foreign direct investment as governments in other regions. Hence, the third objective of this study is to analyse the interaction between corporate tax burdens and actual foreign direct investment flows for selected territories in the Asia-Pacific Region and India.

Company Taxation Regimes in the Asia-Pacific Region, India, and Russia (Chap. 2)

A comparison of the company tax regimes in the Asia-Pacific region, India, and Russia reveals differences in the tax system, the types of taxes relevant for corporations, the respective tax bases and a remarkable variation in corporation tax rates. The lowest rate is levied in Hong Kong (16.5%) whereas Japan and India tax corporate profits at a rate of 30%. The corporation tax is complemented by surcharges in India, Japan, and South Korea and by local profits taxes in Japan and the Philippines. Besides the tax rates, the regulations governing the tax base, e.g. depreciation allowances granted for tax purposes, are an important determinant of the country-specific tax system. Some territories (especially Hong Kong) grant generous allowances for tax purposes whereas other territories are more restrictive. With respect to non-profits taxes borne by corporations the majority of territories levy either a real estate tax or a property tax on business assets. Yet, these capital taxes account for a much lower share of the overall tax burden than profits taxes.

Effective Tax Burden on Domestic and Cross-Border Investments (Chap. 3)

Since location decisions for subsidiaries of multinational investors are usually made for highly profitable investments, the EATR constitutes the relevant measure in the context of this study.

With respect to *domestic investments* the quantitative analyses indicate considerable variations among EATR in the territories considered. EATR is lowest in Hong Kong with 10.3% and highest in Japan with 42.1%. Therefore the spread between the lowest and the highest taxed territory in terms of EATR is 31.8% points and the average EATR of the Asia-Pacific region, India, and Russia is 25%. These results cannot be traced back to one single feature of the tax system. The concept of effective tax levels is conceived to take the interrelation of profits taxes, taxes on capital and the relevant rules concerning depreciation, valuation of inventories and interest deductibility into account. Nonetheless, the results indicate that the statutory tax rate remains the dominant factor in determining the effective average tax burden if the taxation of shareholders is disregarded. Moreover, the overall tax level depends on the mode of finance of the investment and the assets invested in.

EATR of a domestic investment (subsidiary level)

Territory	EATR (%)
Australia	28.3
Cambodia	18.3
China	23.9
Hong Kong	10.3
India	40.0
Indonesia	26.8
Japan	42.1
Malaysia	22.3
Philippines	31.9
Russia	21.7
Singapore	15.9
South Korea	22.5
Taiwan	22.1
Thailand	26.9
Vietnam	22.7

With respect to *cross-border investments* the interaction of national tax regulations, withholding taxes levied in the host territories of the subsidiaries and the method for avoiding international double taxation in the home country of the parent corporation is taken into account. In order to draw general conclusions on the attractiveness of the territories considered for multinational investors, the location of the parent corporation is placed within the United States, where the credit method is applied, or within Germany, where the exemption method is used. The results show that the location of the parent corporation matters for the effective average tax level of the outbound investment and for the ranking of potential investment locations.

The EATR at the level of the German parent still reveals a great variation among the host territories of the subsidiaries. Compared to the EATR at subsidiary level, the average value rises from 25 to 31% which is due to withholding taxes levied on repatriated dividends, to the qualification of 5% of dividends as non-deductible expenses in Germany, as well as to the fact that repatriated interest payments are subject to the German corporation tax level. From the perspective of a German investor, the EATR is highest on outbound investments to Japan (47.7%) and lowest on outbound investment to Hong Kong (11.8%). Overall, only six of the fifteen locations considered bear a lower tax burden on German outbound investments than the German domestic investment.

EATR on German and US outbound investments to the Asia-Pacific region, India, and Russia (parent company level)

Territory	EATR	
	German outbound investment (%)	US outbound investment (%)
Australia	38.3	31.9
Cambodia	29.3	30.6
China	31.5	31.7
Hong Kong	11.8	28.8

(continued)

Territory	EATR	
	German outbound investment (%)	US outbound investment (%)
India	42.5	40.9
Indonesia	34.1	32.2
Japan	47.7	41.6
Malaysia	23.7	30.3
Philippines	38.7	39.6
Russia	26.3	33.3
Singapore	17.3	29.9
South Korea	27.1	31.1
Taiwan	37.9	37.0
Thailand	34.2	32.3
Vietnam	24.1	30.7

Concerning the EATR on US outbound investments to the locations, the effective tax levels are much less dispersed than the EATR on domestic investments or on German outbound investments. Due to the application of the credit method on dividends, location specific comparative advantages of low tax rates are offset. From the perspective of a US investor, the EATR is highest on outbound investments to Japan (41.6%) and lowest on outbound investment to Hong Kong (28.8%). Overall, twelve of the fifteen locations bear a lower tax burden on US outbound investments than the US domestic investment.

Due to different methodologies of avoiding double taxation on dividends and interest payments as well as differences in the applicable withholding tax rates, it is evident that the EATR at the level of the parent corporation depends on the sources of finance of the subsidiary. Except for outbound investments to Japan, the most tax efficient financing strategy of a German or US investor is profit retention at the subsidiary level. In contrast, the German and US investor can largely avoid the higher tax level in Japan by financing the Japanese subsidiary by debt. A US investor or any other investor located in a country that applies the credit method on dividends is indifferent between financing the subsidiary by new equity or debt as long as he can credit the local taxes and the withholding taxes on dividends against the tax liability at home. However, regarding the risk associated with the investment some investors might consider debt financing as more flexible in terms of withdrawing capital from abroad.

Impact of Incentives (Chap. 4)

Most territories in the Asia-Pacific region, India, and Russia grant various tax incentives. In total, our survey revealed 46 major tax incentives. For specified industries, sectors, or regions, the incentives include reductions of the taxable income (i.e. the tax base), the tax rates (i.e. reduced rates and tax holidays) and the tax liability (i.e. a tax credit). The incentives have a significant impact on the ranking of the territories from the highest to the lowest EATR. Moreover, since profits from foreign investments (i.e. dividends) are 95% exempt from taxation in Germany, a multinational German parent company also benefits from the incentives if the profits are transferred to Germany. Especially India and Thailand, where very attractive tax holidays are offered, show a significant decrease of tax burden and advance by five and four positions in the ranking respectively.

In the case of a US parent company the impact is not as substantial, which is due to the credit method. Only where there is excess credit without the application of tax incentives, the tax burden can be reduced. This is mainly the case for India; since the effective average tax rate without incentives is rather high, a reduction also reduces the excess credit and accordingly the overall tax burden.

Six territories, namely Australia, Malaysia, the Philippines, Singapore, Taiwan, and Thailand, offer tax incentives for group structures, especially for the establishment of headquarters. Such incentives mainly include a tax exemption of qualifying income or a reduction of the corporation tax rate.

EATR on German and US Outbound Investments to the Asia-Pacific Region, India, and Russia (Parent Company Level) Considering Tax Incentives for the Year 2009

	EATR	
	German outbound investment (%)	US outbound investment (%)
Australia	38.4	31.9
Cambodia	13.6	30.2
China	20.7	30.8
Hong Kong	11.8	28.8
India	24.3	31.5
Indonesia	31.1	29.2
Japan	47.7	41.6
Malaysia	12.8	29.9
Philippines	30.8	34.2
Russia	24.3	31.6
Singapore	7.5	29.9
South Korea	19.1	30.7
Taiwan	37.9	37.0
Thailand	18.9	30.3
Vietnam	11.7	30.0

Tax Planning Strategies (Chap. 5)

The exploitation of Asian markets is becoming more and more interesting for multinational companies. In order to save taxes when undertaking such investments, it is important to focus on tax planning strategies. Since in most cases the location decision of the investment is already made, it is important to examine whether a certain financing or holding structure can reduce the tax burden.

For a German parent company, it can be shown that withholding taxes can be reduced by setting up a holding company in a territory where tax treaties offer lower withholding tax rates and where repatriated profits are exempt from taxation. Of the territories, Hong Kong, Singapore, Malaysia, and Russia show such characteristics.

Different financing structures can reduce the tax burden as interest payments are deductible from taxable income. But thin capitalisation rules have to be kept in mind. Another favourable strategy is to establish a financing company receiving interest payments and repatriating those in the form of dividends.

In the case of a US parent company, the main objective is to avoid excess credits on repatriated funds. This can be achieved by a good mix and a tax efficient timing of dividend distribution from the foreign subsidiaries, since the US apply an overall limitation so that high creditable taxes can be compensated by low creditable taxes from another territory. Also debt financing reduces the excess since withholding tax rates on interest are in all cases lower than the US corporation tax rate.

Corporate Taxation and Foreign Direct Investment Flows (Chap. 6)

This chapter focuses on the interaction between corporate taxation including special investment incentives and foreign direct investment flows to East Asia. In the period between 1990 and 2007, corporate income tax rates in East Asia have declined significantly on average, albeit not as much as in the EU. At the same time, all countries under consideration have used various special investment incentives to attract investment. Our analysis has shown that flows of foreign direct investment to East Asia are affected by differences in the corporate tax burden and, in particular, special investment incentives. The results indicate that lowering the corporate income tax rate by 1% point increases FDI by 5%. Our results for the impact of special investment incentives imply that FDI in sectors with special tax incentives is 28% larger than without special incentives. This result underlines the importance of tax features besides statutory rates for investment decisions. One should take into account, however, that these results may also have a different interpretation: The presence of FDI in a sector may increase the likelihood that special investment incentives are introduced.

Chapter 1
Motivation for and Structure of the Study

The Asia-Pacific region as well as India, and Russia have gained economic power among the world's economies and offer enormous sales opportunities for multinational companies. Hence, these territories are going to have increasing importance as a trade and investment partner. When considering a foreign direct investment in those territories, the specific taxation framework constitutes one determinant to be accounted for in the decision making process of the multinational investor. Yet, the tax systems in these territories tend to be very complex, especially when considering the incentives offered. At the same time, they are strongly connected to the fast paced development process of the territories themselves, resulting in a sequence of more or less profound tax reforms.

Against this background, the objective of this study is threefold. Firstly, the study is to provide a comparative analysis of the tax systems in 13 territories of the Asia-Pacific region plus India and Russia. Secondly, based on the information collected in the course of the qualitative analysis, reliable information on the effective tax burdens in the territories is to be put forward. Effective tax burdens are relevant for investors' decisions on location, scale and mode of finance of a potential investment. The calculation of the effective tax levels will be based on the approach of Devereux and Griffith (1999). This approach allows condensing the most relevant provisions of tax regimes to a broadly accepted indicator of the attractiveness of a location in terms of tax burden.

The following territories are covered by this study:

• Australia	• Indonesia	• Singapore
• Cambodia	• Japan	• South Korea
• China	• Malaysia	• Taiwan
• Hong Kong	• Philippines	• Thailand
• India	• Russia	• Vietnam

The relevant information on the tax systems of these territories was collected in collaboration with PricewaterhouseCoopers. For this purpose, a questionnaire was conceived covering the most important tax regulations for corporations as well as tax incentives available. The questionnaires were filled out by members of the

D. Endres et al. (eds.), *Company Taxation in the Asia-Pacific Region, India, and Russia*,
DOI 10.1007/978-3-642-12217-0_1, © Springer-Verlag Berlin Heidelberg 2010

regional offices of PricewaterhouseCoopers in the considered territories.[1] The tax regulations refer to the fiscal year 2009.

In recent decades, governments across the world have become increasingly concerned about the impact of taxes on international investment flows. In Europe, the significant decline in corporate tax rates which occurred during the last two decades is widely seen as reflecting the forces of corporate tax competition. In East Asia, governments are at least as concerned about attracting foreign direct investment as governments in other regions. Hence, the third objective of this study is to analyse the interaction between corporate tax burdens and actual foreign direct investment flows for the above listed territories except Australia, Cambodia, Japan, Russia and Vietnam.

The study consists of six chapters. Chapter 2 provides a comparative analysis of the company tax systems in the Asia-Pacific region, India, and Russia. In this context, similarities and particularities with respect to types of profits taxes and non-profits taxes, level of tax rates, elements of the tax base and integration of company taxation into personal taxation will be pointed out. Chapter 3 comprises a short methodological outline of the Devereux and Griffith approach as well as the computation and interpretation of the effective tax levels. For the computation of effective tax burdens, a two-tier approach is chosen. The first step focuses on the effective tax burden of domestic investments in the territories. This analysis will provide insights into the weights of the respective tax drivers and how they explain the cross-territory differences in the effective average tax rates. In a second step, the analysis will be extended by taking withholding taxes and the methods to avoid international double taxation of repatriated profits at the level of the parent company into account. Double taxation on dividends can be avoided either by the exemption method or the tax credit method. Therefore, Germany (exemption method) and the United States (tax credit method) will be considered as locations of the multinational investor. Chapter 4 provides an overview of important tax incentives granted by the territories in the Asia-Pacific region, India, and Russia. For selected typical incentives, the impact on the effective tax burden will be computed. Chapter 5 will illustrate some relevant tax planning strategies for investments in the Asia-Pacific region. Chapter 6 focuses on the interaction between corporate tax burdens and actual foreign direct investment flows.

[1] In addition the IBFD Database (IBFD (2009)) and PricewaterhouseCoopers Worldwide Tax Summaries (PricewaterhouseCoopers (2008)) were used.

Chapter 2
Company Taxation Regimes in the Asia-Pacific Region, India, and Russia

2.1 Overview

Generally, as regards the fiscal year 2009, the tax systems in the Asia-Pacific region, India, and Russia follow international standards. In the majority of territories considered, resident corporations are taxed on their worldwide income. In Hong Kong and Malaysia, the definition of taxable income is based on the territoriality principle. In these territories, profits are only taxable if derived from domestic sources. Singapore taxes income based on the concepts of territoriality and receipt. With respect to the integration of the corporation income tax into the personal income tax of the individual shareholders, about half the territories operate a classical system. Referring to the rate structure, the applicable nominal corporation tax rates vary considerably within the Asia-Pacific region, India, and Russia. The lowest rate is levied in Hong Kong (16.5%) whereas Japan and India tax corporate profits at a rate of 30%. The corporation tax is complemented by surcharges in India, Japan, and South Korea and by local profits taxes in Japan and the Philippines. Besides the tax rates, the regulations governing the tax base, e.g. depreciation allowances granted for tax purposes, are an important determinant of the territory-specific tax systems. Some territories (especially Hong Kong) grant generous allowances for tax purposes whereas other territories are more restrictive. Turning to non-profits taxes borne by corporations the majority of territories levy either a real estate tax or a property tax on business assets.

2.2 Corporation Tax Systems

There are various types of corporation tax systems in the Asia-Pacific region, India, and Russia. Regarding the extent of integration of the corporation tax into the personal income tax of the individual shareholder, three main categories can be

D. Endres et al. (eds.), *Company Taxation in the Asia-Pacific Region, India, and Russia*,
DOI 10.1007/978-3-642-12217-0_2,

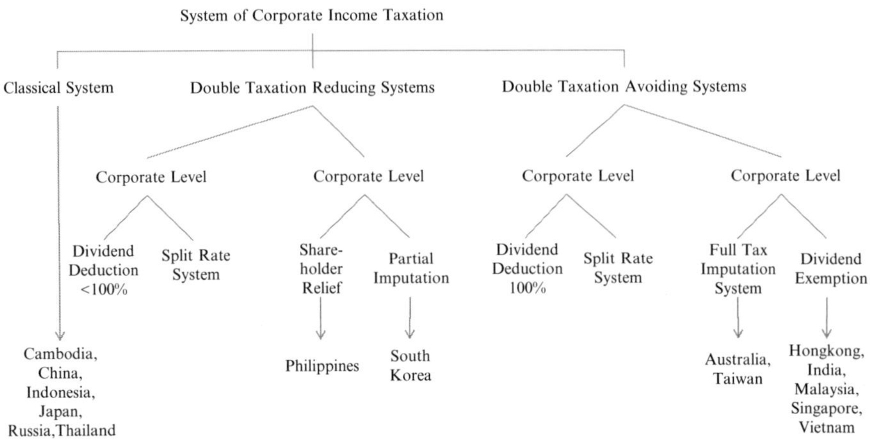

Fig. 2.1 Systems of corporate income taxation in the Asia-Pacific region, India, and Russia

distinguished: the classical system, double taxation reducing systems and double taxation avoiding systems. Figure 2.1 classifies the territories according to the corporation tax system implemented.

The classical system leads to double taxation on dividends by imposing both corporation tax and personal income tax. Cambodia, China, Indonesia, Japan, Russia, and Thailand apply a form of the classical system.

In contrast to the classical system, double taxation avoiding systems ensure that profits are only taxed once – either at the corporate level or at the shareholder level. Both Australia and Taiwan operate a full imputation system, where dividends can be "franked" at the company level with an imputation credit and individual shareholders are required to gross up their dividend income for received imputation credits and use this credit as an offset against their personal income tax liability. Consequently, there is full relief from corporation tax on distributed profits and dividends are subject to personal income tax only.

As another way to eliminate double taxation, Hong Kong, India, Malaysia, Singapore, and Vietnam operate a system of dividend exemption at the shareholder level under which profits are subject only to corporate income tax. Notably, there is a transition period in Malaysia from 1 January 2008 to 31 December 2013 where companies may opt for the old imputation system instead of the newly introduced one-tier corporate tax system. As a result, for these four territories, the corporation tax rate determines the tax burden of both retained and distributed profits.

In order to reduce the economic double taxation on dividends, South Korea implements a partial imputation system in which 12% of the dividend income can be credited against personal income tax liability. The Philippines, by contrast, grant a reduced final withholding tax rate of 10% instead of 32% for dividend income of individual shareholders.

Since the relief for corporation tax is granted only to domestic shareholders, the type of corporation tax system is only relevant if a subsidiary has resident shareholders. From the perspective of a multinational investor, the local tax burden in the considered location is decisive as well as the tax burden on repatriated profits, i.e. withholding taxes and the method to avoid international double taxation.

2.3 Tax Rates

Table 2.1 illustrates nominal corporation tax rates as well as surcharges and local business tax rates on profits if applicable. The effective statutory profits tax rate is a combined tax rate that comprises corporate income taxes, surcharges and local taxes on profits. The effective statutory tax rate also takes the interrelation of different profits taxes (e.g. deductibility of one profits tax from the tax base of another) into account. The average combined statutory profits tax rate[1] on distributed profits is 26.9% and the spread between the highest and the lowest rate amounts to 28.7% points. The combined statutory profits tax rate is lowest in Hong Kong (16.5%) and highest in India (45.2%). In India, companies face an additional "dividend distribution tax" of 15%. Thus the tax rate on distributed profits largely exceeds the tax rate on retained earnings. The reverse holds true for Taiwan. Taiwan also operates a "split-rate" tax system but in contrast to India levies an additional "retained earnings tax" on undistributed profits.

In all countries with the exception of Japan, Malaysia, Singapore, South Korea, and Taiwan, the corporation tax rate is proportional. In Japan, the standard rate is 30%; however, a special tax rate of 22% is applicable to taxable income of first JPY 8 million (59,435.67 €)[2] on condition that the paid-in capital of the company is equal to or less than JPY 100 million (742,945.91 €). Similarly a special tax rate of 20% on the first MYR 500,000 (98,699.15 €) of taxable income is available in Malaysia for corporations with a paid-in capital of less than MYR 2.5 million (493,495.73 €). In Singapore, South Korea, and Taiwan, the corporation tax rate follows a progressive rate structure regardless of the amount of paid-in capital. As for Singapore, the nominal corporate tax rate is 18% but a 75% exemption applies to the first SGD 10,000 (3,690.99 €) and a 50% exemption applies to the next SGD 290,000 (107,038.72 €). In South Korea, the tax rate in the first income bracket which is defined by a taxable income of up to KRW 200,000,000 (115,604.43 €) is taxed at 11% whereas the excess income is taxed at 22%. Taxable income up to

[1]The combined statutory profits tax rate includes the corporation tax as well as surcharges and local profits taxes. The deductibility of surcharges or local profits taxes for corporation tax purposes is accounted for.

[2]For exchange rates see Table A.1.

Table 2.1 Corporation tax rates and statutory tax rates (%)

Territory	Nominal corporation tax rate	Surcharge	Local profits tax rate (nominal)	Effective statutory profits tax rate
Australia	30	–	–	30
Cambodia	20	–	–	20
China	25	–	–	25
Hong Kong	16.5	–	–	16.5
India	40.5/30	13.3	–	45.21/33.99
Indonesia	28	–	–	28
Japan	30	20.7	7.67	40.75
Malaysia	25	–	–	25
Philippines	30	–	0.75	30.53
Russia	20	–	–	20
Singapore	18	–	–	18
South Korea	22	10	–	24.2
Taiwan	25/32.5	–	–	25/32.5
Thailand	30	–	–	30
Vietnam	25	–	–	25
Average	25.6/25.5			26.9/26.6
Germany	15	5.5	14.98	30.81
USA	35	–	8.84	38.83

India. The nominal corporation tax rate on retained earnings is 30%. Distributed profits are subject to an additional dividend distribution tax of 15%. A surcharge of 10% applies if income exceeds INR 10 m (143,363.42 €). An education cess of 3% also applies on the tax payable (including surcharge)
Japan. The inhabitants' tax of 20.7% is levied on the amount of national corporation tax as a surcharge. There are three additional local taxes which are deductible from corporate income tax. The enterprise tax is levied on the corporate income at a rate of 3.26%. The local corporate tax is 148% of the enterprise tax. A local business tax of 0.48% applies on the value added of the current year
Philippines. Local tax is levied on the annual turnover and is deductible from corporate income tax. The local tax rate is 0.75% in Manila
South Korea. A local surtax of 10% is levied on the corporation tax liability
Taiwan. The corporation tax rate of 25% applies to distributed profits. After-tax retained earnings are subject to an additional "retained earnings tax" at 10% thus yielding a combined statutory profits tax rate on retained earnings of 32.5% (=25% + 10% × (1–25%))
USA. The state profits tax rate of California is the example. In addition to the federal tax and the state tax, a manufacturing deduction for domestic production activities of 6% is taken into account (35% × (1–6%) + 8.84% × (1–35% × (1–6%)) = 38.83%)

TWD 50,000 (1,027.55 €) is exempt in Taiwan. In the second bracket, ranging from TWD 50,000 (1,027.55 €) to TWD 100,000 (2,055.11 €), the applicable rate on the total income is 15%. Any excess income is subject to 25% corporate income tax.

India, Japan, and South Korea levy important surcharges on the corporation tax payable. In India, corporations face a surcharge of 10% on the corporation tax if income exceeds INR 10 million (143,363.42 €) and an education contribution of 3% on the tax payable (including surcharge). Japanese companies are subject to a "Prefectural and Municipal Inhabitants Tax". In Tokyo, this surcharge amounts to 20.7%. South Korea also imposes a local "Inhabitants Tax" as a surcharge of 10% on the corporate tax liability.

Only Japan and the Philippines levy additional local taxes. In Japan, there are currently three additional local taxes which are deductible from the corporate income tax. Altogether they amount to 7.67%. A so-called enterprise tax is imposed on the corporate income at a rate of 3.26%. The local corporate tax is 148% of the enterprise tax and a local business tax of 0.48% applies to the value added of the current year. The Philippines impose a local tax on the annual turnover at a rate of 0.75% in Manila.

2.4 Tax Bases

In all territories, the profits liable to corporation tax are determined on the basis of national financial accounting standards and are adjusted to a different extent to obtain the corporation tax base. All territories have in common that the tax base is based upon the accrual principle. Since the regulations governing the tax base might differ significantly from one territory to another, the aim of this section is to take a closer look at important elements of the taxable income, most of which are taken into account in the calculation of effective tax burdens in Chap. 3. Table 2.2 gives an overview of the regulations implemented into the model.

2.4.1 Industrial Buildings

Generally, industrial buildings are valued at acquisition costs. In all territories, industrial buildings can be depreciated for tax purposes. The useful life ranges from 20 to 50 years. In the majority of territories, industrial buildings must be depreciated at a straight-line basis. The declining-balance method is only applicable in India and Taiwan. The Philippines usually allow the sum of the years' digits method[3] for depreciation of industrial buildings; thus the annual depreciation rate varies from year to year. Initial allowances in the first period are granted in Hong Kong (20%), Malaysia (10%), and Singapore (25%) in addition to an annual allowance at a straight-line basis. In Russia, 10% of acquisition costs can be deducted in the first period and the standard straight-line depreciation rate is applied in subsequent years.

2.4.2 Intangibles

In all territories, expenditures for intangibles (e.g. patents) that have been acquired against payment from a third party have to be capitalised and amortised either over their useful life, or as stated in the tax law. Intangibles are treated most favourably

[3]The sum of the years' digits method is an accelerated depreciation method. The numerator of the depreciation rate is the remaining useful life and the denominator equals the sum of the years' digits, i.e. 21 ($1 + 2 + 3 + 4 + 5 + 6 = 21$) if the useful life is 6 years.

Table 2.2 Depreciation and amortisation of assets and valuation of inventories

Territory	Industrial buildings			Intangibles[a]			Machinery[b]			Inventory valuation
	Method	Rate (%)	Length (years)	Method	Rate (%)	Length (years)	Method	Rate (%)	Length (years)	
Australia	SL	4	25	SL	5	20	DB	28.57	ufd	Weighted average
Cambodia	SL	5	20	SL	10	10	DB	20	ufd	Weighted average
China	SL	5	20	SL	10	10	SL	10	10	Weighted average
Hong Kong	SL	24	1	SL	100	1	SL	100	1	Weighted average
		4	19							
India	DB	10	ufd	DB	25	ufd	DB	35	1	Weighted average
								15	ufd	
Indonesia	SL	5	20	DB	12.5	ufd	DB	12.5	ufd	Weighted Average
Japan	SL	2.63	38	SL	12.5	8	DB	25	7	FIFO
							SL	33.33	3	
Malaysia	SL	13	1	SL	20	5	SL	34	1	Weighted average
		3	29					14	4	
								10	1	
Philippines	SD	var	30	SD	var	10	SD	var	7	Weighted average
Russia	SL	10	1	SL	10	10	SL	30	1	LIFO
		3.1	29					11.67	6	
Singapore	SL	28	1	SL	20	m	SL	33.33	3	Weighted average
		3	24							
South Korea	SL	2.5	40	SL	10	10	DB	45.1	ufd	LIFO
Taiwan	DB	4.5	50	SL	10	10	SL	14.29	7	LIFO
Thailand	SL	5	20	SD	var	10	SD	var	7	LIFO
Vietnam	SL	3.33	30	SL	10	10	SL	14.29	7	LIFO
Germany	SL	3	33.3	SL	20	5	SL	14.29	7	LIFO

USA	SL	2.46	1	SL	6.66	15	DB	14.29	1	LIFO
		2.56	38				DB	24.49	6	
		0.11	1				SL	8.92	1	

The kind of capital allowances and valuation of inventories represent the most tax efficient possibility; other possibilities are ignored. If multiple methods and rates are given, they represent the development of depreciation allowances over the lifetime of the asset. *DB* declining balance method, *SD* sum of years' digit method, *SL* straight-line method, *ufd* until fully depreciated, *FIFO* first-in-first-out, *LIFO* last-in-first-out, *var* varying depreciation rate

Hong Kong. An immediate 100% first year allowance is granted for machinery that qualifies as prescribed fixed assets, e.g. machinery or plant used specifically and directly for any manufacturing process, and for expenditure on patents provided that the rights are not purchased wholly from an associate

India. New plant and machinery acquired by a company engaged in manufacturing or production is entitled to an additional depreciation of 20% of the actual cost in the year of acquisition

Malaysia. For buildings and machinery an initial allowance is granted in the first period that amounts to 10/20% of the acquisition cost

Russia. For assets with a useful life of less than 3 years and more than 20 years a deduction equal up to 10% of the acquisition costs of fixed assets is available in the year of acquisition. This rate amounts to 30% for assets with a useful life of more than 3 years and less than 20 years

Singapore. An accelerated depreciation of 33 1/3% is available for plant and machinery. For buildings an initial allowance of 25% is granted

Taiwan. If the declining balance method is used, the residual value of the asset is fixed at 10% of its cost and depreciation is granted throughout its service life on the remaining 90%

Vietnam. Profitable companies are granted accelerated depreciation of machinery. The depreciation rate is twice the depreciation rate under straight line depreciation

[a]The purchase of a patent is assumed. If depreciation depends on the useful life of the patent and no period is specified in the national tax codes, a period of 10 years is assumed for the calculation of the allowance rate

[b]If depreciation depends on the useful life of the machinery and no period is specified in the national tax codes, a period of 7 years is assumed for the calculation of the allowance rate

Table 2.3 Treatment of losses for tax purposes

Territory	Loss carry-forward		Loss carry-back	
	Available	Periods	Available	Periods
Australia	Yes	Indefinite	–	–
Cambodia	Yes	5	–	–
China	Yes	5	–	–
Hong Kong	Yes	Indefinite	–	–
India	Yes	8	–	–
Indonesia	Yes	5	–	–
Japan	Yes	7	Yes	1
Malaysia	Yes	Indefinite	–	–
Philippines	Yes	3	–	–
Russia	Yes	10	–	–
Singapore	Yes	Indefinite	Yes	1
South Korea	Yes	5	Yes, for SME	1
Taiwan	Yes	10	–	–
Thailand	Yes	5	–	–
Vietnam	Yes	5	–	–

in Hong Kong due to an immediate 100% first year allowance. Besides Hong Kong, the average useful life of patents ranges from 5 years in Malaysia and Singapore to 20 years in Australia. In India and Indonesia, intangibles are depreciated according to the declining balance method. The sum of the years' digits method defines the tax depreciation path on the Philippines and in Thailand (Table 2.3).

2.4.3 *Tangible Fixed Assets*

Tangible fixed assets such as plant, machinery, and office equipment can be depreciated in all territories. In Hong Kong, machinery that qualifies as a prescribed fixed asset, e.g. machinery or plant used specifically and directly for any manufacturing process is eligible for an immediate 100% first year allowance. From a tax-minimising perspective, this regulation is by far the most generous compared to the depreciation allowances granted in other territories. Australia, Cambodia, India, Indonesia, Japan, and South Korea allow tangible fixed assets to be depreciated according to the declining balance method. As opposed to the straight-line method, the declining balance method enables the corporation to deduct a higher amount of the acquisition costs in earlier periods, thus reducing the tax burden. Among the countries allowing the declining balance method, only Japan permits a switch-over to the straight-line method once the depreciation expense under the declining-balance method falls below the respective value under the straight-line method. The respective rates for declining balance depreciation might vary according to the predefined useful life of certain types of machinery. For some standard machinery with a medium lifetime, the applicable rates range between 12.5% in Indonesia and 45.1% in South Korea. Machinery is depreciated according to the straight-line method in China, Malaysia, Russia, Singapore, Taiwan, and Vietnam at an allowance rate ranging from 10% in China to 14.29%

in Taiwan and Vietnam.[4] Regardless of the depreciation method applied, an initial allowance of 20% is granted in India and Malaysia. In Russia, 30% of acquisition costs are deductible from the tax base in the year of acquisition if the useful life of the asset ranges between 3 and 20 years. The remaining costs are depreciated according to the straight-line method in subsequent years. As for intangible assets, the Philippines and Thailand apply the sum of the years' digit method for an assumed useful life of machinery of 7 years.

2.4.4 Inventories

Inventories are valued at production cost. The concrete amount at which inventories are included in the accounts depends on the extent to which overhead is allocated to the products. Changes in stock of finished goods and work in progress are valued on the basis of alternative simplifying assumptions. In the majority of territories, the weighted-average cost method prevails for inventory valuation. Russia, South Korea, Taiwan, Thailand, and Vietnam, however, permit the last-in-first-out (LIFO) method. In times of rising prices LIFO is the most tax efficient method. The items most recently purchased at the higher price are matched against taxable revenues. Consequently, the taxable income decreases in earlier periods and payment of corporation tax is deferred. In Japan, the LIFO method as well as the weighted-average cost method are no longer accepted since 2009. Thus the first-in-first-out (FIFO) method is the only method for a simplified valuation of inventories.

2.4.5 Provisions

Due to the diversity of the tax treatment of provisions, it is not possible to provide a comprehensive overview. Rather, the focus is on provisions for bad debts or uncertain (contingent) liabilities. In each of the territories, the creation of provisions or reserves for bad debts is allowed. In Japan, Malaysia, Russia, Singapore, South Korea, and Taiwan, provisions for bad debts are deductible for corporation tax if certain prerequisites are fulfilled. In Malaysia, for example, provisions for bad debts are only deductible if they are specifically identified as irrecoverable.

2.4.6 Losses

All of the territories allow a loss carry-forward. Australia, Hong Kong, Malaysia, and Singapore offer an indefinite loss carry-forward. Among the other territories, the period of loss-carry forward ranges between 3 years on the Philippines and 10 years in Taiwan, and Russia. Cambodia, China, Indonesia, South Korea, Thailand, and

[4] Again a standard machinery with a medium useful life is assumed.

Vietnam allow a loss carry-forward for 5 periods. Slightly more attractive loss regulations offer Japan with 7 years and India with 8 years. Japan, Singapore, and South Korea even grant a loss carry-back of one period. In South Korea, however, the loss carry-back is only available for small and medium sized corporations.

2.4.7 Interest Deductibility

Interest expenses are generally deductible if incurred for the production of services or goods. Yet, several territories restrict the extent to which interest payments can reduce the tax base. In Cambodia, interest payments can only be deducted up to an amount that equals the total interest income plus 50% of non-interest income of the year. On the Philippines, the amount of deductible interest expenses is reduced by 42% of the company's taxable interest income. In Russia and Taiwan, interest expenses are only deductible if the interest rates do not exceed predefined thresholds. In Russia the threshold is based on similar loans. In Taiwan, the threshold is set by the ministry of finance.

2.5 Non-Profits Taxes for Corporations

In addition to corporation tax on profits and local business taxes on profits, companies may be subject to certain non-profits taxes. In Table 2.4, the nominal tax rates already account for possible valuation effects of the taxable asset. The effective tax rates, in contrast, account for the deductibility of real estate tax or other property taxes from corporate income tax.[5]

A real estate tax is levied in China, India, Indonesia, Japan, Singapore, South Korea, Taiwan, and Thailand. The taxable value is derived either from the market value, a standardised value or from the rental value. The effective tax rates range from an almost negligible 0.1% in Indonesia to a more substantial 1% in Thailand and 1.6% in India.

Japan, the Philippines, and Russia levy a property tax on fixed assets. In contrast to real estate tax, these property taxes are also levied on other fixed assets than real estate. The market value or a standardised value represents the taxable base for the respective property taxes. In Japan, land, buildings, and depreciable assets are subject to an effective property tax of 0.8%. Russia imposes a property tax on all fixed assets except intangibles. The rate is subject to regional variations, e.g. in Moscow, the effective tax rate on property is 1.8%. On the Philippines, the property

[5]Other indirect taxes, e.g. stamp tax or duties, are not considered as the study only examines direct taxation of profits. Real estate and assets tax are usually deductible from the corporate tax base and can therefore have an impact on the tax burden of profits.

Table 2.4 Summary of nominal and effective tax rates on property and real estate (%)

Territory	Real estate tax		Property tax	
	Nominal[a]	Effective[b]	Nominal[a]	Effective[b]
Australia	–	–	–	–
Cambodia	–	–	–	–
China	0.96	0.72	–	–
Hong Kong	–	–	–	–
India	2.48	1.63	–	–
Indonesia	0.2	0.14	–	–
Japan	0.3	0.18	1.4	0.83
Malaysia	–	–	–	–
Philippines	–	–	2.4	2.4
Russia	–	–	2.2	1.76
Singapore	0.5	0.41	–	–
South Korea	1.06	0.8	–	–
Taiwan	1.5	1.01	–	–
Thailand	1.0	0.7	–	–
Vietnam	–	–	–	–
Germany	0.39	0.27	–	–
USA	–	–	1.0	0.62

China. Real property tax is imposed on the original cost net of allowance deduction which ranges from 10 to 30%. In this study a deduction of 20% is assumed

Hong Kong. Corporations carrying on a business in Hong Kong can apply for an exemption from property tax or a credit against corporate tax if property is used by the company for producing the profits chargeable to profits tax

India. The law on real estate tax varies from one state to another. In the state of Karnataka, the applicable tax rate on real estate is 31% (including surcharge). The net annual value of the property is approximated with 8% of acquisition cost. Real estate tax is deductible for corporation tax purposes. An additional net wealth tax is levied on the aggregate value of specified assets but any assets used for conducting business are exempt

Indonesia. The actual tax due is calculated by applying the tax rate of 0.5% to the assessment value of taxable property. The assessment value of taxable property is determined as a percentage of the deemed fair market value. It is 40% for any land or building which have a sale value of more than IDR 1 billion (70,634.92 €)

Japan. Property tax is levied on real estate property as well as depreciable assets at a rate of 1.4%. Moreover city planning tax is imposed on land and buildings at a rate of 0.3%

Philippines. Real property tax is based on the assessed value of the property. It is determined based on the fair market value of the real property multiplied by the assessment level. For buildings the assessment level varies between 30 and 80% according to the value of the building. In this study an assessment level of 80% is assumed. For industrial machinery the assessment level is 80%. The nominal rate is 2% for Manila. In addition to the real property tax, a 1% Special Education Fund is levied on the same tax base

Russia. The corporate property tax is imposed on the average aggregate annual depreciated value of fixed assets. The rate is 2.2% for Moscow

Singapore. Property tax of 10% is imposed on the annual value of all immovable properties. In this study a rental value of 5% of acquisition cost is assumed as annual value

South Korea. The tax base is the current standard value of the industrial building. It is assumed that the current standard value corresponds to the acquisition costs. The rate is 2.5% in the first five periods (regulation for newly built factory) and 0.5% afterwards

Taiwan. Building tax is levied annually on the taxable present value of the building. For registered factories which are used for manufacturing 50% of the market value are taxable. The rate is 3% for commercial usage of buildings

Thailand. The tax base is the assessed economic rental value of the building. It is assumed to be 8% of acquisition costs. The nominal rate is 12.5%

USA. A net wealth tax is imposed on tangible assets, i.e. on industrial buildings and machinery. The tax rate may not exceed 1%. The tax base is the market value

[a]The nominal tax rate already accounts for possible valuation effects

[b]The effective rate accounts for the deductibility of real estate tax from corporate income tax

tax is levied on real estate and industrial machinery at an effective rate of 2.4%. It is not deductible from corporate income tax.

2.6 Conclusion

A comparison of the company tax regimes in the Asia-Pacific region, India, and Russia reveals differences in the tax system, the types of taxes relevant for corporations, the respective tax bases and – above all – a remarkably great variation in corporation tax rates. The impact of the different taxes, tax rates and tax bases on the effective tax burdens differs according to the type of investment, the source of finance and the profitability of an investment. A qualitative comparison of the different elements of the tax regimes cannot identify their impacts on the effective tax burdens. It is therefore unclear as to whether favourable allowances in the tax base compensate for higher tax rates and vice versa. Therefore the following quantitative analysis will determine the effective average tax levels at the subsidiary level and the parent company level in the different territories. Moreover, the analysis will provide insights into the weights of the respective tax drivers and how they explain the cross-territory differences in the effective average tax burdens.

Chapter 3
The Effective Tax Burden on Domestic and Cross-Border Investments in the Asia-Pacific Region

3.1 Methodology and Assumptions

The intention of the quantitative analysis is to reveal the incentives of the tax systems in the Asia-Pacific region, India, and Russia with regard to location decisions, investment strategies and financing options for subsidiaries. The commonly accepted methodology of Devereux and Griffith (See Devereux and Griffith (1999) and Schreiber et al. (2002)) can provide reliable information on this issue and is therefore relied on in this study. This approach is a so-called forward-looking approach, calculating the tax burden on a hypothetical investment project of a company. Based on the approach of Devereux and Griffith, the European Commission carried out comprehensive surveys on the comparison of effective tax burdens in the EU (See Devereux et al. (2008) and European Commission (2001)). The model applied in this study on the Asia-Pacific region, India, and Russia is the same as the one used by the European Commission.[1] An important strength of this methodology is the possibility of modelling the most relevant provisions of tax regimes in a systematic way. The model of Devereux and Griffith is explicitly conceived to compute the effective tax burden not only on marginal investments (effective marginal tax rate – EMTR) but also on highly profitable investments (effective average tax rate – EATR). Since location decisions for subsidiaries of multinational investors are usually made for highly profitable investments, the EATR constitutes the relevant measure in the context of this study.[2] When computing the EATR, the most important regulations of the tax regimes in the Asia-Pacific region, India, and Russia are accounted for. Besides the regulations which determine the local tax burden borne in the potential locations of the subsidiary, territory

[1]Since it is described in detail in the 2001 report of the European Commission, it is not explained in detail here.

[2]The EMTR, in contrast, provides insights in the allocation efficiency of tax regimes.

D. Endres et al. (eds.), *Company Taxation in the Asia-Pacific Region, India, and Russia*,
DOI 10.1007/978-3-642-12217-0_3, © Springer-Verlag Berlin Heidelberg 2010

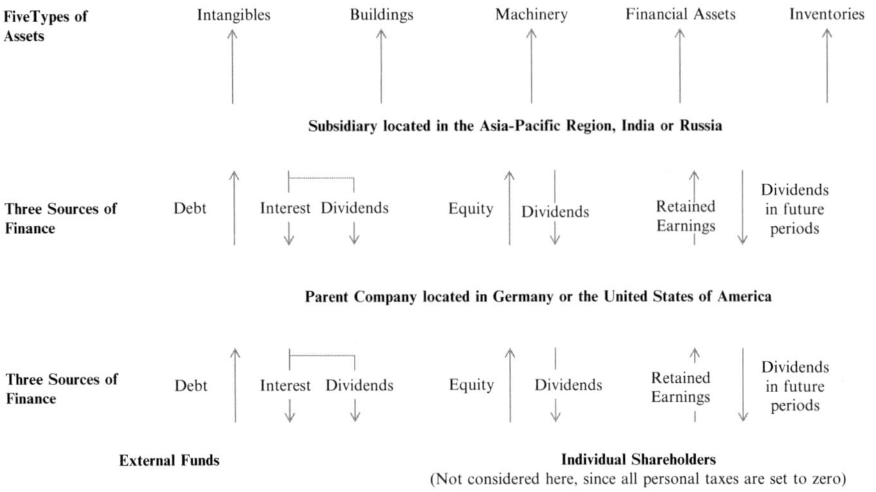

Fig. 3.1 Set-up of the investment, assets and sources of finance

specific withholding taxes on profit repatriation and methods for avoiding international double taxation in the investor's home territory are accounted for in the calculations. The following section briefly outlines the underlying assumptions on investment and financing strategies and the tax provisions covered by the model.

Figure 3.1 illustrates the set-up of the model investment. For the calculations it is assumed that a parent company is resident either in Germany or in the United States. Hence, the analysis captures both, the perspective of a multinational investor located in a country that applies the exemption method to avoid double taxation of dividends (Germany) and the perspective of a multinational investor located in a country that applies the tax credit method (the United States).

The shareholders of the parent corporations are private portfolio investors residing in the same country as the parent. The investment of the parent company takes place in a subsidiary located in the Asia-Pacific region, India or Russia. As subsidiary, the model assumes a company of the manufacturing sector taking the legal form of a corporation. The subsidiary can invest in five different assets: intangibles acquired against payment from third parties, industrial buildings, machinery, financial assets, and inventory. The types of assets are weighted equally. The subsidiary is wholly owned by the parent corporation. Thus only a direct cross-border investment is considered. The funds to finance the investment of the subsidiary are provided by the parent corporation. The funds consist of 55% retained earnings, 10% new equity and 35% debt. The subsidiary disregards the options of raising funds in local or international capital markets. Profits earned in the subsidiary are entirely repatriated to the parent. In case of financing by retained earnings this means that retained profits are distributed in subsequent periods. In case of debt financing, it is assumed that the subsidiary pays interest to the parent at a fixed rate and distributes the remaining profits as dividends. Under these

Table 3.1 Summary of the underlying assumptions

Assumption on ...	Value
Legal form	Corporation
Industry	Manufacturing sector
Assets (weight)	Industrial buildings (20%), intangible assets (20%), machinery (20%), financial assets (20%), inventories (20%)
Sources of finance (weight)	*Subsidiary*: retained earnings (55%), new equity (10%), debt (35%) *Parent*: retained earnings (33.33%), new equity (33.33%), debt (33.33%)
True economic depreciation	Declining balance method Industrial buildings 3.1% Intangibles 15.35% Machinery 17.5%
Real interest rate	5%
Pre-tax real rate of return	20%
Inflation rate	2%

assumptions, profits derived from the investment in the Asia-Pacific region, India, and Russia may be taxed at three different levels: In the first place, the earnings of the investment are taxed at the level of the subsidiary. Secondly, the parent might face an additional tax burden when profits are repatriated. The individual shareholders of the parent company represent the third potential level of taxation. In the following analysis, however, the taxation of dividends, capital gains and interest income at the level of the individual shareholder is not taken into account, since personal taxation is in most cases not relevant for investment and location decisions of multinationals. Table 3.1 summarises the most important model assumptions of the following calculations. The assumptions correspond to the respective assumptions applied in the surveys of the European Commission (See Devereux et al. (2008) and European Commission (2001)). Hence, the results derived for the Asia-Pacific region, India, and Russia can directly be compared to the respective results for the EU countries.

The approach applied in this study covers the most relevant tax provisions of the national tax systems in the Asia-Pacific region, India, and Russia. With regard to the taxation of corporate profits, it considers nominal corporation tax rates, regional taxes on profits, surcharges as well as some special rates for particular types of income and expenditure. Moreover, real estate taxes, property and net-wealth taxes are accounted for. Generally, the calculations assume a level of corporate profits and capital that falls within the top-bracket of statutory tax rates. Regarding the definition of the tax base, the calculations incorporate the relevant rules concerning depreciation and amortisation for three types of assets (buildings, intangibles acquired from third parties and machinery), valuation of inventories and interest deductibility in case of debt financing. The impact of selected tax incentives is also assessed. If regulations are of optional character, the most tax efficient regulation is chosen. As regards the repatriation of profits in a cross-border setting (see Sect. 3.3), territory specific withholding taxes and the method to avoid international double taxation at the level of the parent company are taken into account. The calculations are based on the tax regulations as of 1 January 2009.

3.2 The Effective Tax Burden at the Level of the Subsidiary (Domestic Investment)

3.2.1 Overall Tax Burden

This section presents estimates of effective tax burdens at the level of the subsidiary. Taxes borne by the parent company in the host territory of investment (i.e. withholding tax rates) and in the home territory (i.e. taxes on repatriated profits) are therefore set at zero here. Hence, the EATR borne at the level of the subsidiary equals the EATR of a domestic investment when shareholder taxation is disregarded. This allows identification of the tax drivers inherent in each domestic tax system. Figure 3.2 illustrates the dispersion of effective average tax rates in the locations. The EATR is by far the lowest in Hong Kong with 10.3%. Singapore (15.9%) and Cambodia (18.3%) are ranked second and third. Russia, Taiwan, Malaysia, South Korea, Vietnam, and China constitute a group of six territories with very similar effective average tax burdens that range from 21.7% in Russia

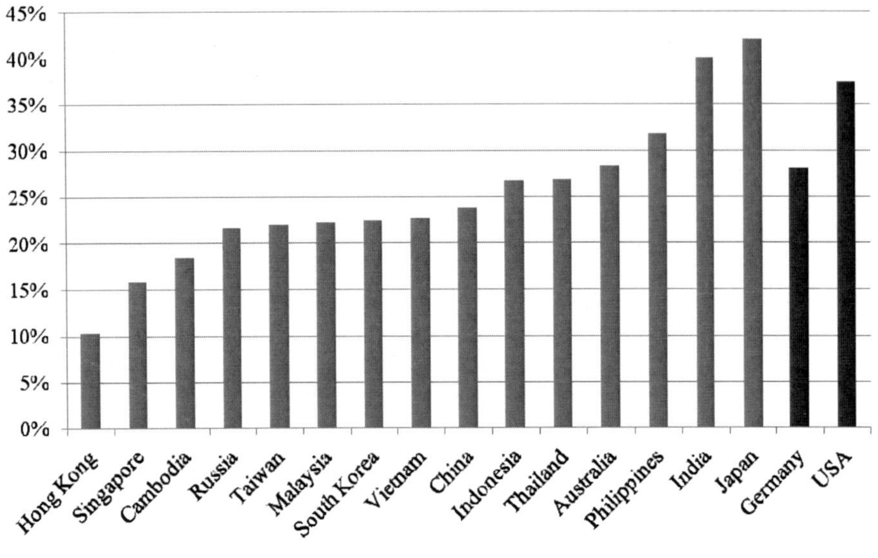

Fig. 3.2 Effective average tax rates (subsidiary level); see Table A.2

to 23.9% in China. In all these territories, the EATR is below the average of the Asia-Pacific region, India, and Russia which is 25.3%. In Indonesia (26.8%) and Thailand (26.9%) the EATR is above average. The effective tax burden is remarkably high in India (40%) and Japan (42.1%). These results indicate an enormous spread of 31.8% points between the lowest and the highest taxed territory in terms of EATR.

Figure 3.2 also illustrates the EATR on domestic investments in Germany (28.1%) and the United States (37.4%). The comparison to the tax level in the Asia-Pacific region, India, and Russia indicates that – as regards the EATR on domestic investments – the tax burden is in most of the Asia-Pacific locations, and Russia lower than in Germany and the United States. Especially Hong Kong, Singapore, and Cambodia turn out to be very favourable in terms of tax burden. Yet, the taxation of the multinational investment, considering also withholding taxes and the method to avoid double taxation at the level of the parent company has still to be taken into account. This will be done in Sect. 3.3.

The results described above cannot be traced back to one single feature of the tax system. The concept of effective tax levels is conceived to take the interrelation of profits taxes, taxes on capital and the relevant rules concerning depreciation, valuation of inventories and interest deductibility into account. Nonetheless, the results displayed in Fig. 3.3 indicate that the statutory tax rate remains the dominant factor in determining the effective average tax burden if the taxation of shareholders is disregarded.

Since a profitable investment is assumed, the relative weight of depreciation allowances and non-profits taxes declines with the increasing importance of profits taxes. This becomes intuitively clear, when two investment projects are compared

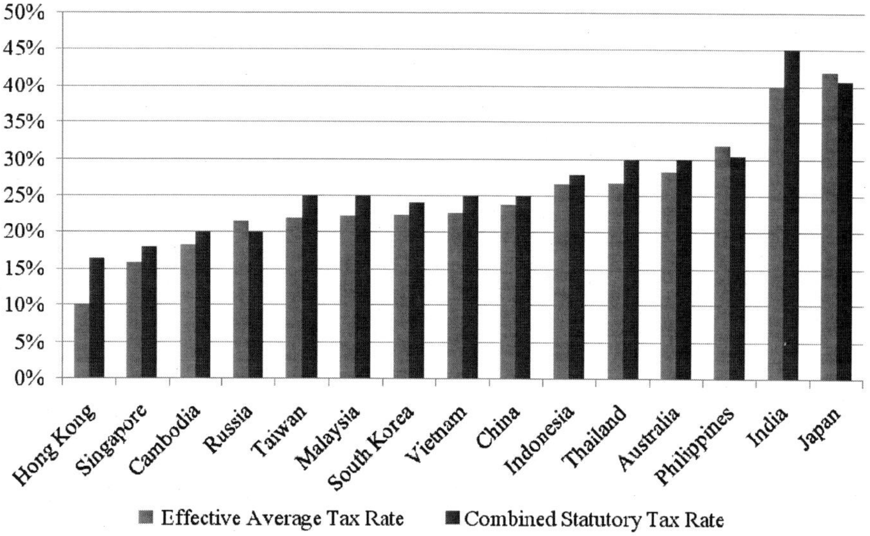

Fig. 3.3 Effective average tax rates and statutory corporate tax rates (subsidiary level)

that require identical expenses but differ in return. In case of the investment with the higher profitability, the receipts exceed the expenses by a higher amount. Thus, the treatment of these expenses for the purpose of taxation, e.g. the path of tax depreciation allowances, is relatively less important. The additional income is regularly taxed at the statutory tax rate without triggering additional allowances. To sum up, the treatment of regulations governing the tax base becomes less relevant for the determination of the effective tax burden if the level of profitability increases. The same holds true for non-profits taxes. Still, the definition of the tax base and non-profits taxes explain the deviation of the EATR from the combined statutory tax rate.

In the majority of territories, the EATR is lower than the combined statutory tax rate due to the tax-reducing impact of the tax base (e.g. depreciation and inventory valuation) and the deduction of interest payments in the case of debt financing. Yet, for Russia, the Philippines, and Japan, the average tax burden of the investment exceeds the combined statutory tax rate on profits. These countries levy an important share of non-profits taxes that increases the tax burden of the investment.

The spread between EATR and the combined statutory tax rate is in most cases below 3% points. Hong Kong and India are the exceptions. Both territories show a remarkably high spread between the EATR and the combined statutory tax rate that exceeds 6% points. In Hong Kong, the low EATR can be traced back to especially generous depreciation regulations, i.e. the one-off depreciation for machinery and intangibles and the tax exemption of interest income from deposits with authorised institutions. Due to these generous regulations, the ordinary return of the investment remains largely untaxed and only rents are subject to the combined statutory tax rate. In India, the difference between the EATR and the combined statutory tax rate can be attributed to the split corporate tax rate. The combined statutory tax rate of 45.2% is levied on distributed profits. The tax rate on retained earnings, in contrast, is only 34%. If a part of the profits is retained in each year – as has been assumed for the calculations – this results in an interest and liquidity gain that reduces the EATR.

3.2.2 Impact of Different Sources of Finance

In this section, the impact of different financing policies on the effective tax burden on domestic investments is analysed. Figure 3.4 presents the territory specific EATR for three different sources of finance: retained earnings, new equity and debt.

Since interest payments are completely or at least partly deductible at the corporate level, debt financing of an investment is privileged compared to equity finance. From the perspective of a corporation located in one of the locations, debt financing therefore constitutes the most tax-efficient financing strategy. This conclusion, however, does not necessarily hold true if the level of the parent corporation is accounted for. Since different regulations might apply for the taxation of cross border interest payments and repatriated profits, the optimal financing strategy

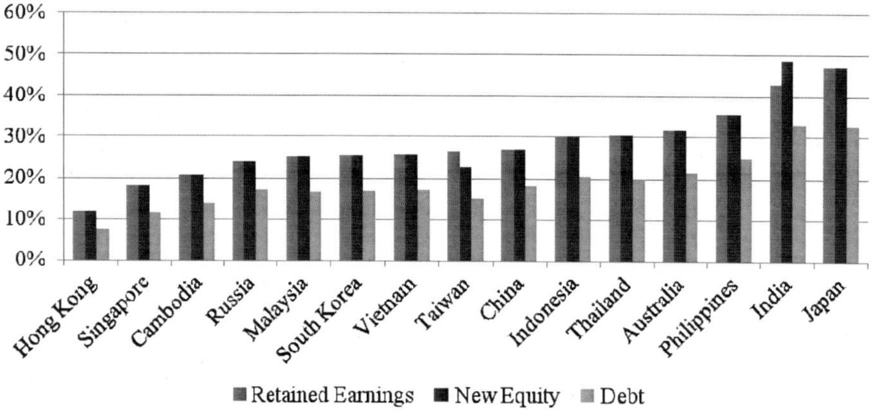

Fig. 3.4 Effective average tax rates and sources of finance (subsidiary level); see Table A.2

might differ compared to the domestic case. Section 3.3 will analyse financing strategies of a parent corporation in more detail.

All territories except for India and Taiwan do not differentiate between the taxation of retained earnings and the taxation of distributed profits, i.e. the same tax rate is applied on profits regardless of whether they are distributed or retained. Therefore, the EATR at the corporate level on investments financed with retained earnings are equal to those on investments financed with new equity. India and Taiwan, in contrast, operate a split-rate tax system with regard to the taxation of retained and distributed profits. India levies an additional tax on dividend distributions and thus privileges investments financed with retained earnings, whereas Taiwan encourages new equity finance by taxing retained earnings higher than distributed profits. Hence, the most tax efficient way of financing the investment by equity differs in these territories. In India, taxation can be partly deferred by profit retention at the corporate level. This results in interest and liquidity gains. Earnings derived on an investment project in Taiwan, in contrast, are treated more favourably if distributed. Therefore, new investments financed by new equity bear a lower tax burden.

3.2.3 Impact of Different Types of Investment

To illustrate how the choice of assets influences the EATR of an investment, the following considerations are based on the assumption that 100% of funds are invested in the acquisition of one type of asset. Figure 3.5 summarises the results. There is a remarkable spread of the asset specific EATRs resulting from different accounting rules for different kinds of assets. The main drivers of these findings tend to be specific depreciation regulations and non-profits taxes on certain assets. It is striking that many locations in the region encourage investments in machinery

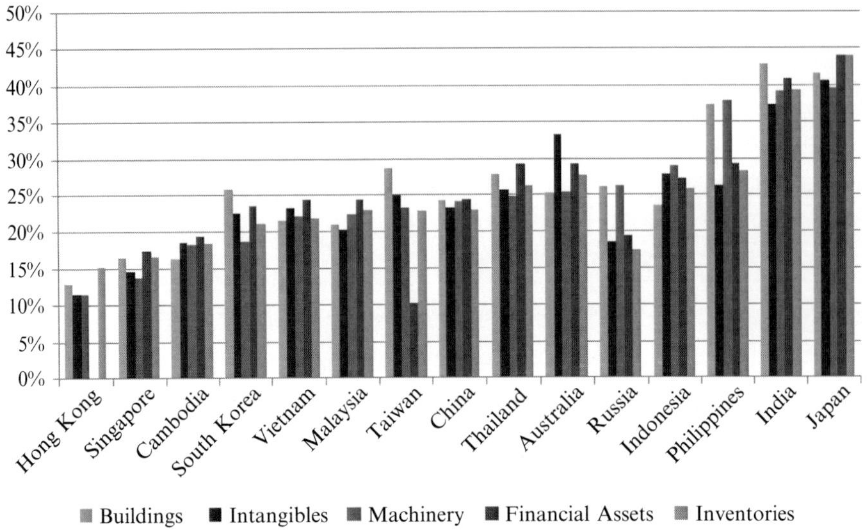

Fig. 3.5 Effective average tax rates and types of assets (subsidiary level); see Table A.2

and/or intangibles by granting generous depreciation allowances. For machinery, these regulations are remarkably generous in Hong Kong (one-off depreciation), India (20% initial depreciation), Singapore (3 year depreciation), and South Korea (declining balance 45.1%). With regard to the taxation of investment in intangible assets, Hong Kong, Malaysia, Singapore, India, Thailand, and China offer depreciation regulations that allow a higher deduction than necessary.

The EATR on buildings is usually higher than the EATR on other assets if territories levy real estate taxes or property taxes on buildings. In some territories, especially Indonesia, the impact of real estate tax is partially mitigated by generous depreciation rules for buildings. Since the Philippines and Russia levy a property tax on buildings and machinery, the EATR on both assets is comparably high in both countries. In Japan, all assets are subject to a property tax resulting in a high level of EATR for all assets.

The earnings derived from financial assets are directly subject to the statutory tax rate and the regulations determining the tax base are irrelevant in the context of financial assets. A special regulation applies to Hong Kong: Since interest income derived from any deposit placed in Hong Kong with an authorised institution is tax-exempt, the resulting EATR is zero. In Taiwan, the EATR on financial assets is low, since specified interest income is subject to a final withholding tax of 10% as opposed to the combined statutory tax rate of 25% on distributed profits.

With regard to inventories, the impact of inflation on the EATR becomes evident. Inflation increases the nominal sales price and nominal costs. Only the last-in-first-out method avoids the taxation of inflationary gains and therefore results in a lowest EATR for inventories. Using the first-in-first-out and weighted-average-cost method, taxable income is measured by the difference between nominal sales price and nominal cost valued at a lower price level. Thus, especially in case the first-in-first-out method is applied, e.g. in Japan, the taxable income rises with inflation.

To sum up, Fig. 3.5 illustrates that the effective tax burden depends on the asset composition of the investment. The ranking of locations might therefore change if different weight distributions are attributed to the considered set of assets. As an example, locations on the Philippines would improve their ranking if an investment with a smaller share of machinery and higher share of intangible assets was considered.

3.3 The Effective Tax Burden on Cross-Border Investments

3.3.1 General Approaches to the Taxation of Cross-Border Investments

So far, the analysis considered only the tax burden borne at the level of the subsidiary in order to illustrate territory specific tax drivers. The taxation of profit repatriation has been explicitly excluded in that step. Yet, the taxation of cross-border dividends and interest payments becomes relevant if the multinational investor considers the overall tax burden of alternative cross-border investments. Therefore, the following analysis takes the interaction of national tax regulations, withholding taxes levied in the host territories of the subsidiaries and the method for avoiding international double taxation in the home country of the parent corporation into account. With regard to the methods avoiding international double taxation, one can differentiate between the exemption method and the credit method which are both set out in Article 23 of the OECD Model Convention.

In the event of debt financing, the accepted approach for the taxation of cross-border interest payments is the credit method. Interest paid by a foreign subsidiary is, in general, deductible from the taxable profits of the subsidiary and subject to corporation tax at the level of the parent company. Consequently, foreign profits repatriated as interest payments bear – regardless of the location of the subsidiary – the same tax burden as domestic investments of the parent corporation (capital export neutrality). Hence, debt financing of the foreign subsidiary is only tax efficient if the tax level in the home territory is lower than in the host territory of the investment. A withholding tax levied on interest payments is credited against the domestic corporation tax and thus usually does not result in an extra tax burden.

Turning to cross-border investments financed by equity, territories either apply the exemption method or the credit method in their double taxation conventions. If the exemption method is used, double taxation is avoided by taxing profits only at the level of the subsidiary and exempting repatriated dividends in the hands of the parent corporation. Therefore, the tax burden borne at the level of the parent company in principle equals the tax burden at subsidiary level, if withholding taxes are disregarded (capital import neutrality). Hence, from the perspective of a multinational investor resident in an exemption country, the tax burden borne at the level of the subsidiary largely determines the comparative advantage of one location against another. If the credit method is applied, in contrast, double taxation of dividends is avoided by crediting profits taxes borne at the level of the subsidiary against the domestic corporation tax on the underlying profits at the level of the parent corporation. If the foreign tax level is below the domestic tax level, the tax burden on foreign dividends is thus grossed-up to the domestic level. Consequently, a multinational investor cannot benefit from lower taxes abroad if profits are distributed. Since the foreign tax credit on dividends is usually limited to the domestic corporation tax on the underlying profits, the tax burden at the level of the parent company constitutes the minimum tax burden that the multinational investor faces. The overall tax burden of the investment exceeds the level of the parent company if the foreign tax level is higher.

Whether withholding taxes on dividend payments will result in a definite tax burden depends on whether the exemption method or the credit method is applied. In case of the exemption method, the levying of dividend withholding taxes always results in a definite tax burden. In the event of the credit method, dividend withholding taxes only become definite if they – together with the foreign corporation tax – exceed the domestic tax level.

In this study, Germany and the United States will be considered as possible home countries of the multinational investor. Hence the analysis includes both the perspective of a country applying the exemption method (Germany) and the perspective of a country applying the credit method (United States) to avoid the double taxation of foreign dividends. Moreover it can be determined whether the concrete location of the parent corporation and, thus, the home country's tax system has an impact on the comparative attractiveness of the analysed regions as investment destinations.

Figure 3.6 outlines the tax burden associated with different financing strategies and methods to avoid double taxation in case of equity finance. Before examining the situation of a German and a US investor in more detail (see the following Sect. 3.3.2), some general conclusions on the most tax-efficient financing strategies will be drawn.

If the subsidiary reinvests its profits, it will be the only taxpayer. The effective tax level in the host territory determines the optimal location choice.

If profits are repatriated to the parent company, the optimal tax planning strategy depends on the relationship between the level of foreign taxes (i.e. taxes borne at the level of the subsidiary and withholding taxes on dividends) and the level of domestic taxes in the home country of the parent company (Germany or the United States). Where the foreign taxes exceed the corporation tax rate in the home country, debt financing of the subsidiary is more tax efficient than equity financing regardless of the method which is applied to avoid double taxation. The reason is twofold. On the one hand, in case of the credit method, there is no refund of an excess tax credit (but only carry forward of excess credit would be allowed). On the other hand, a withholding tax levied on dividends results in a definite tax burden whereas withholding tax on interest is creditable against domestic taxes. Whenever foreign taxes are lower than the corporation tax rate in the home country of the

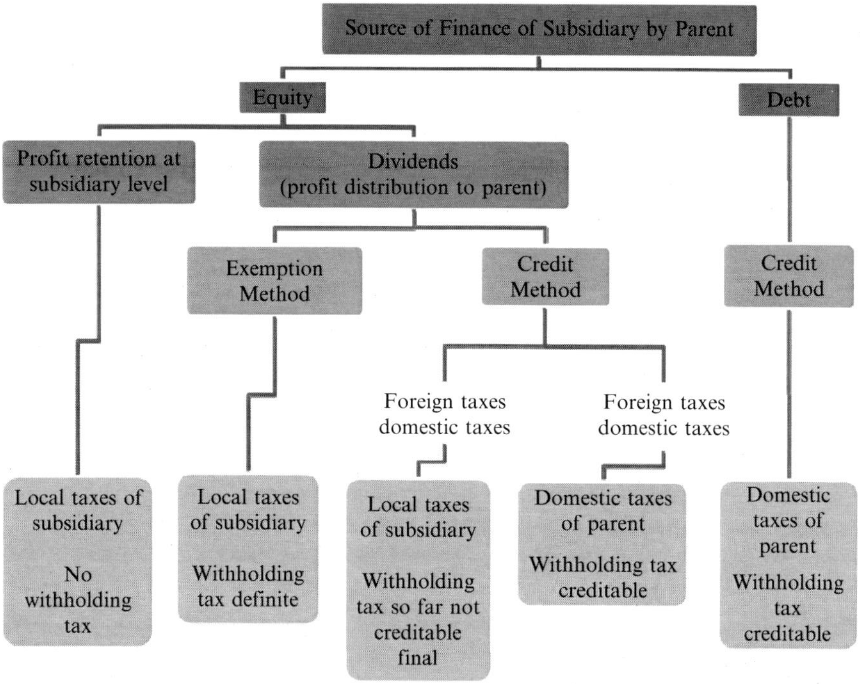

Fig. 3.6 Taxation of cross-border income depending on the source of finance

parent company, the optimal financing strategy depends on the method of avoiding double taxation applied. For the German multinational (or any other multinational located in an exemption country) equity-financing of the foreign subsidiary is more tax efficient than debt financing since the investor can thus benefit from the lower foreign tax levels as determined in Sect. 3.2. The respective withholding tax on dividends however, becomes absolute. Considering the United States as the home country for the multinational investor, the effective tax burden on debt financing and equity financing are generally the same, since the tax burden on foreign dividends is grossed-up to the domestic level and withholding taxes are creditable against domestic taxes.

In this context it has, however, to be taken into account that the amount of available tax credits as well as the determination of the applicable tax credit limitation is complex and depends on the specific underlying fact pattern. For the purpose of the following analyses it is assumed that the available tax credits connected to the foreign source income equals to the respective foreign income taxes (taxes assessed at the level of the foreign subsidiaries and incurred withholding taxes). The foreign tax credit limitation shall be determined by applying the nominal US Federal Tax Rate on the foreign source income. Deviations, for example, with respect to the underlying Earnings and Profits, tax pools and the foreign tax credit limitations which may exist depending on the actual facts and circumstances are not considered.

3.3.2 Situation of a German Parent Company and a US Parent Company

3.3.2.1 Taxation of Cross-Border Dividend Flows and Interest Payments

In the event of debt financing, the taxation of cross-border interest payments is based on the credit method, regardless of the location of the parent company. Interest paid by a foreign subsidiary is generally deductible from the profits of the subsidiary and subject to corporation tax at the level of the parent company. The withholding tax on interest levied abroad is credited against corporation tax. Table 3.2 shows that except for Hong Kong or Russia, all territories levy withholding taxes on interest payments to German or US parent corporations. The withholding tax rate is highest on interest payments received from Taiwan (20%).

As regards the taxation of repatriated dividends, Germany and the United States apply different regimes. At the level of the German parent company, dividend payments from both domestic and foreign subsidiaries are exempt from corporation tax and trade tax. However, 5% of the dividends received are considered as non-deductible business expense and are therefore subject to corporation tax, solidarity surcharge and trade tax. At the level of the US Parent Company, the foreign tax on dividend payments is credited against the domestic corporation tax on the underlying profits. If the foreign tax level exceeds the domestic corporation tax in the United States, an excess credit is not refunded thus resulting in a final burden.

Withholding taxes on dividends may not be credited against the German corporation tax and are therefore final. Withholding taxes on dividends repatriated to the United States can be credited if the foreign tax level (consisting of local country income taxes and withholding taxes) is below the level of corporate taxation in the US. By contrast, if the foreign tax level is higher, the withholding tax becomes a final

Table 3.2 Withholding taxes on dividends and interest paid to a German or US parent company

Territory of the subsidiary	Parent company in Germany		Parent company in the US	
	Dividends	Interest	Dividends	Interest
Australia	15	10	0	10
Cambodia	14	14	14	14
China	10	10	10	10
Hong Kong	0	0	0	0
India	0	10	0	15
Indonesia	10	10	10	10
Japan	10	10	0	10
Malaysia	0	15	0	15
Philippines	10	15	15	15
Russia	5	0	5	0
Singapore	0	8	0	15
South Korea	5	10	10	12
Taiwan	20	20	20	20
Thailand	10	15	10	15
Vietnam	0	10	0	10

burden. The withholding tax is zero on dividends distributed to Germany or the United States from Hong Kong, India, Malaysia, Singapore, and Vietnam. In addition, a zero withholding tax rate applies on dividends paid by a subsidiary in Australia or Japan to a parent company in the United States. The highest withholding tax rate on dividends distributed from the locations under review to Germany or the United States is again levied in Taiwan. Where the withholding tax is final, it will increase the tax burden on equity financing of the subsidiary in the territory.

3.3.2.2 Overall Tax Burden

Figure 3.7 illustrates the aggregate EATR on German outbound investments to the considered locations in the Asia-Pacific region, India, and Russia. In addition, the EATR on the respective domestic investment in Germany is outlined for reasons of comparison.

The EATR at the level of the German parent still reveals a great variation among the host territories of the subsidiaries. Compared to the EATR at subsidiary level, the average value rises from 25.3 to 31.3%. On the one hand, this increase is due to withholding taxes levied on repatriated dividends. On the other hand, repatriated interest payments are subject to the German corporation tax level.

From the perspective of a German investor, the EATR is highest on outbound investments to India (42.5%) and Japan (47.7%). In contrast, Fig. 3.7 reveals Hong Kong (11.8%) and Singapore (17.3%) as the by far most attractive locations for German outbound investment. This result is on the one hand driven by very low

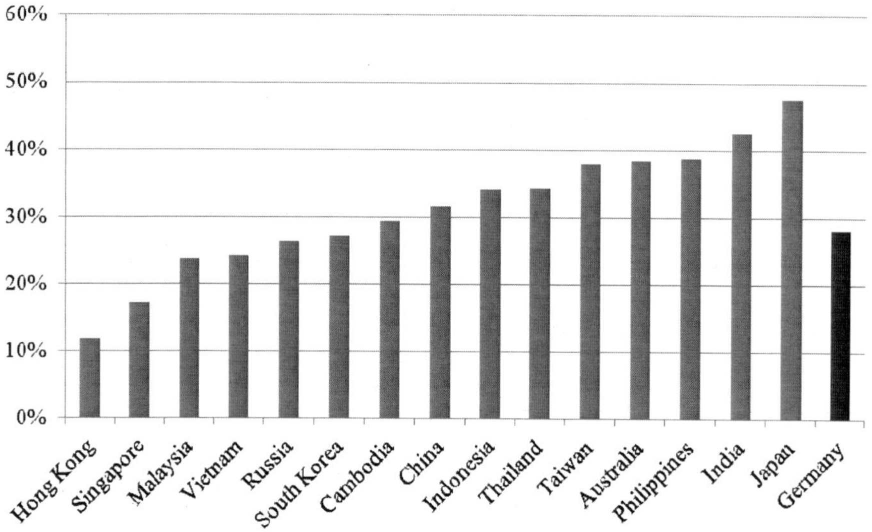

Fig. 3.7 Effective average tax rates of German outbound investments to the Asia-Pacific region, India, and Russia (parent company level); see Table A.3

domestic tax levels in Hong Kong and Singapore which are reflected by low EATRs on domestic investments (see Fig. 3.2). On the other hand, both territories do not levy withholding taxes on dividends distributed to the German parent corporation that would result in an additional tax burden. Yet, the EATR on the cross-border investment increases slightly compared to the domestic result since repatriated interest payments are subject to German tax.

Hong Kong and Singapore apart, all territories experience a significant deterioration of their attractiveness for German outbound investments when withholding taxes are taken into account. The increase from the EATR on domestic investments to the EATR on outbound investments from Germany is especially high for Cambodia (11% points) and Taiwan (15.8% points), since both territories levy substantial withholding taxes on dividends.

Overall, only six of the fifteen considered locations bear a lower tax burden on German outbound investments than the German domestic investment. Again, this illustrates that the attractiveness of the each location is influenced not only by its national level of taxation but also strongly by withholding taxes on dividends which become a final tax burden due to the application of the exemption method in Germany.

Figure 3.8 illustrates the EATR on US outbound investments to the locations in the Asia-Pacific region, India or Russia. Not surprisingly, the effective tax levels turn out to be much less dispersed than the EATR on domestic investments (Fig. 3.2) or the EATR on German outbound investments (Fig. 3.7).

This finding is a typical outcome of applying the credit method for the taxation of foreign dividends. Since the minimum tax on dividends equals the federal

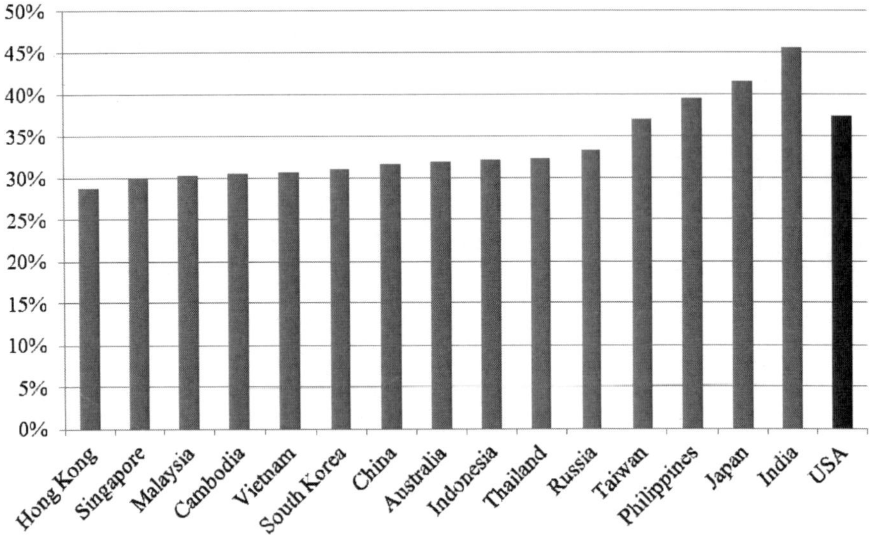

Fig. 3.8 Effective average tax rates of US outbound investments to the Asia-Pacific region, India, and Russia; see Table A.4

corporate tax level in the United States (35%), location specific comparative advantages of low tax rates are offset. Yet, the tax base regulations (e.g. generous depreciation regulations) as well as non-profits taxes that are not creditable against US tax liability still matter for the ranking of territories. Consequently, Hong Kong and Singapore are associated with the lowest tax burden on US outbound investments. However, their position is much less dominant than in case of German outbound investments.

For the majority of locations considered, the EATR on outbound investments from the United States ranges between 28.8% (Hong Kong) and 37% (Taiwan). The effective tax levels in these territories are still below the EATR of domestic investments in the United States[3] (37.4%) since the investment is partially financed by retained earnings, thus deferring to some extent the repatriation of dividends and the taxation at higher US profits tax rates to the future.[4] This effect is negligible for Taiwan, since the split corporate tax rate implies a higher tax burden on retained earnings. From the perspective of an investor in the United States, investments in subsidiaries located in the Philippines, Japan, and India bear a higher tax burden than the domestic investment, at least if a weighted financing strategy is considered. This is due to an excess tax credit that is not repayable thus resulting in a definite tax burden and to non creditable non-profits taxes.

Table 3.3 summarises the EATR on German and US outbound investments to the Asia-Pacific region, India, and Russia, and illustrates the respective ranking of subsidiary locations. For both, German and US investors, Hong Kong, Singapore, and Malaysia represent the most attractive locations as regards the overall tax

Table 3.3 Comparison of effective average tax rates on German and US outbound investments and respective ranking of subsidiary locations

Subsidiary in	German parent corporation		US parent corporation	
	EATR (%)	Ranking	EATR (%)	Ranking
Australia	38.4	12	31.9	8
Cambodia	29.3	7	30.6	4
China	31.5	8	31.7	7
Hong Kong	11.8	1	28.8	1
India	47.2	14	45.6	15
Indonesia	34.1	9	32.2	9
Japan	47.7	15	41.6	14
Malaysia	23.7	3	30.3	3
Philippines	38.7	13	39.6	13
Russia	26.3	5	33.3	11
Singapore	17.3	2	30.0	2
South Korea	27.1	6	31.1	6
Taiwan	37.9	11	37.0	12
Thailand	34.2	10	32.3	10
Vietnam	24.1	4	30.7	5

[3]The state profits tax of California is considered.

[4]The model allows deferring the distribution by one period.

burden of the investment. Yet, other locations, e.g. Australia and Cambodia, are more attractive for the US investor than for the German investor. Apart from domestic tax levels at the subsidiary, withholding taxes levied on dividends largely influence the attractiveness of subsidiary locations from the perspective of a German investor, since they result in a final tax burden. The US investor, by contrast, can credit the foreign taxes on repatriated dividends against the domestic taxes, as long as the foreign tax level is lower than the federal corporate tax rate of 35%. Hence, the ranking is much less influenced by the domestic tax level of the subsidiary and the withholding taxes on dividends.

3.3.2.3 Impact of Different Sources of Finance

This section considers how the interaction of the tax regimes in the potential host territories of cross-border investments and the home country of the parent corporation influences the most tax-efficient means of financing the subsidiary. Due to different methods of avoiding double taxation on dividends and interest payments as well as differences in the applicable withholding tax rates, it is evident that the EATR at the level of the parent corporation depends on the sources of finance of the subsidiary. Whereas the previous analysis was based on a weighted financing of the subsidiary by retained earnings, new equity and debt, the following calculations consider each financing strategy in isolation.

Figure 3.9 shows the outbound EATR by source of finance for a German investor and Fig. 3.10 shows the respective values for a US investor.

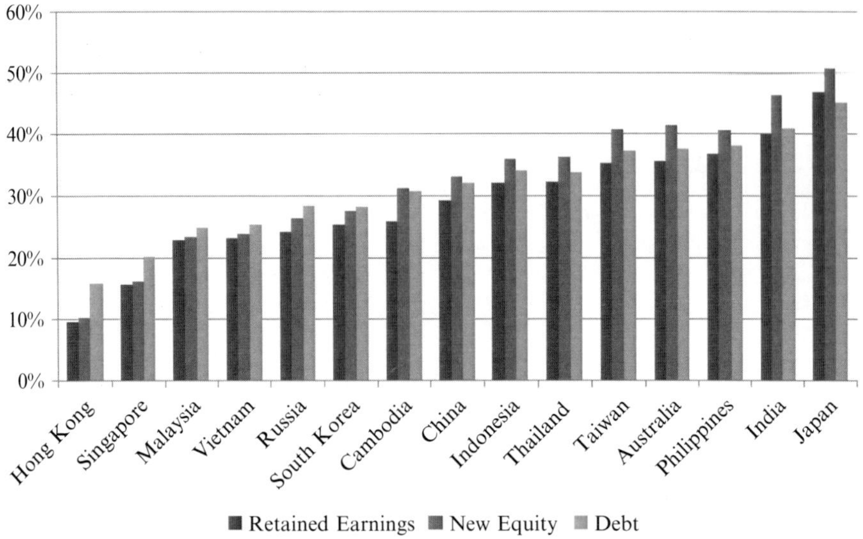

Fig. 3.9 Effective average tax rates on German outbound investments to the Asia-Pacific region, India, and Russia according to the sources of finance (parent company level); see Table A.3

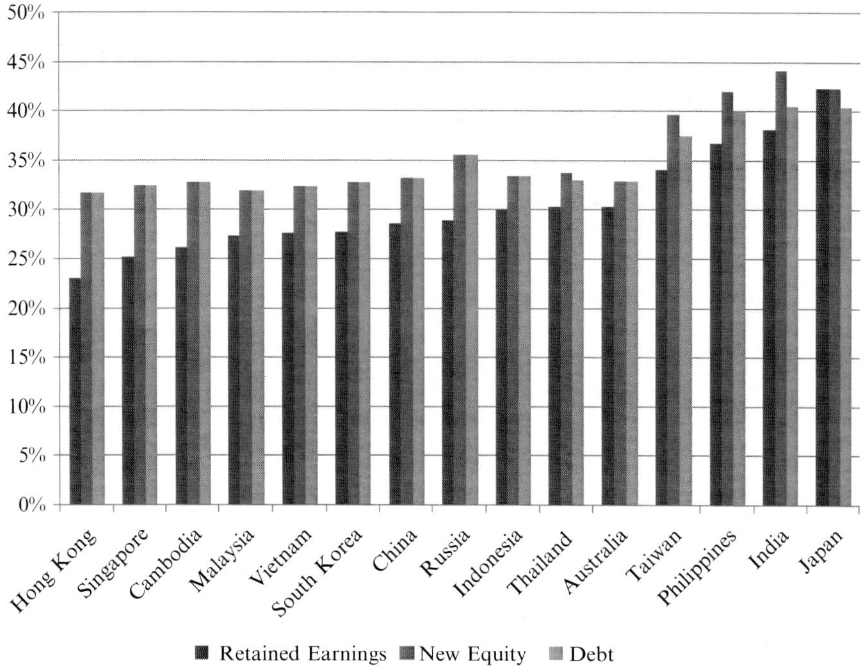

Fig. 3.10 Effective average tax rates on US outbound investments to the Asia-Pacific region, India, and Russia according to the sources of finance (parent company level); see Table A.4

Except for outbound investments to Japan, the most tax-efficient financing strategy of a German or US investor would be profit retention at the subsidiary level. The additional taxes on dividends[5] are deferred until profits are distributed. By contrast, these taxes become final burdens where the subsidiary is financed by new equity. Hence, financing the subsidiary by new equity induces a notably higher overall tax burden than resorting on retained earnings as source of finance. In India, the EATR soars if the subsidiary is financed with new equity instead of retained earnings. This increase in the effective tax burden can be attributed to the additional dividend distribution tax of 17% (including surcharges) payable by Indian companies on distributed profits. With regard to an investment in a subsidiary in Japan, debt financing is the most tax efficient source of finance.[6] By choosing debt financing, the German and US investor can largely avoid the higher local tax level in Japan and the additional withholding taxes on dividends. Due to the credit method, the part of profits that is repatriated to Germany or the United States via interest payments bears the lower tax burden of the home country. Only the exceeding

[5]In the case of Germany, these additional taxes comprise withholding taxes and the taxation of 5% of dividends that are not exempt. In the case of the United States, the taxation of all dividends at US tax rates.

[6]Please note that due to model restrictions, thin-capitalisation regulations cannot be accounted for.

amount of profits is distributed as dividend, thus being subject to the Japanese tax level plus withholding taxes.

Figure 3.10 reveals that a US investor or any other investor located in a country that applies the credit method on dividends is indifferent between financing the subsidiary by new equity or debt as long as he can credit the local taxes and the withholding taxes on dividends against his tax liability at home. In India, Japan, the Philippines, Taiwan, and Thailand, the EATR on equity financed investments exceeds the effective tax burden on debt financed investment since the excess tax credit on dividends is not refunded at the level of the US parent corporation.

The key result of the previous analysis is the significant preference for financing the subsidiary by retained earnings. However, to what extent financing an investment by retained earnings is a feasible strategy also depends on other factors, especially the risk associated with the investment. In this context, the investor might consider debt financing as more flexible in terms of withdrawing capital from abroad.

Chapter 4
Tax Incentives in the Asia-Pacific Region

4.1 Overview of Tax Incentives

It can be shown that Foreign Direct Investment (FDI) has several positive effects on the economy of the host territory. Not only an increase of productivity, but also the training of employees or the transfer of technology are important consequences and can result in economic growth for the particular territory (see Hunya (2006)). As the economic differences between Asian territories are large, there is a lot of tension in the region. In particular, countries like China, India, South Korea, and Japan are among the largest economies in the world. Indonesia, the Philippines, Malaysia, Thailand, and Vietnam are succeeding in establishing long-term growth, but smaller economies can also benefit from capital inflow through foreign direct investment and stabilise their economic growth. So far, cheap labour costs have caused an inflow of manufacturing industries, leading to Asia becoming an important source of automobiles, machinery, and electronics. The statistics show that the Foreign Direct Investment inflow in the territories of this study has almost tripled since 2005 (see UNCTAD (2009)).

Tax incentives have proven their worth as an attraction for inward investment (see de Mooij and Ederveen (2003)). The leading economic territories have, in the past, attracted manufacturing investments by offering tax incentives. Now they are starting to change their focus to high technology industries. Just in 2008, China has changed its tax incentives structure from supporting foreign enterprises to supporting high technology enterprises in general. It is expected that other territories will follow this approach.

Tax incentives have different impacts on the tax burden. They reduce taxable income (i.e. the tax base), the tax rates or the tax liability. Typical reductions on taxable income are accelerated depreciation and tax-free reserves. Accelerated depreciation merely results in a tax deferral. A tax-free investment reserve reduces the taxable base in addition to regular depreciation, which results in a higher tax relief overall. In some territories, reduced tax rates are available for investments in special economic zones (SEZ), for companies receiving the Pioneer Status for

D. Endres et al. (eds.), *Company Taxation in the Asia-Pacific Region, India, and Russia*,
DOI 10.1007/978-3-642-12217-0_4,

investments in certain sectors, or they are offered to foreign investors engaged in qualified projects. Some territories grant tax holidays if certain conditions are fulfilled. A tax holiday means that a company is exempt from taxation for several years. In effect, the tax rate is set to zero for the period for which the tax holiday is granted. Therefore, a tax holiday can be classified as a tax rate reducing incentive over a certain number of years. Some of the territories allow crediting part of the amount invested against the company's tax liability (tax credit) if certain conditions are met.

Overall, our survey revealed 46 major tax incentives. Firstly, we provide a description of the tax incentives available in the territories. Incentives for group structures are described in Sect. 4.4. Secondly, the impact of selected tax incentives on the effective tax burden is calculated using typical tax incentives (bold). Tax incentives have not been considered for all territories, since only investment incentives can be implemented into the model. R&D expenditures cannot be calculated (Australia, Japan). In other cases, the information given was too vague for the incentive to be calculated (Japan). Table 4.1 summarises the tax incentives.

4.1.1 Australia

Tax investment incentives are not provided on a broad basis. Yet, in limited circumstances, incentives are granted on a case-by-case basis. Among other criteria an investment is only eligible for tax incentives if it would otherwise not be accomplished in Australia and if it creates general economic benefit. R&D activities are encouraged by granting a super deduction of 125% if the "aggregated research and development amount" exceeds AUD 20,000. R&D expenditure includes contracted expenditure, salary expenditure and other expenditure. An additional 50% deduction is granted if the company increased the expenditure compared to the average of the previous 3 years.

Since only R&D activities are supported, no incentives are implemented into the model.

4.1.2 Cambodia

Based on the 2003 Investment Act, qualified investment projects which are registered with the Council for the Development of Cambodia are granted several tax incentives that are in part mutually exclusive. Companies can elect to use either a tax holiday or a 40% special depreciation in the first period in addition to the normal depreciation charges on assets used in manufacturing. Depending on the characteristics of the project and the priorities of the government, the tax holiday is granted for a period of 3–6 years. Foreign direct investment can be registered as qualified investment projects if they are not covered by a negative list which

Table 4.1 Summary of general tax incentives in the considered territories

Territory	Reduction in taxable income		Reduction in the tax rate	Reduction in the tax liability	
	Tax deferral	Tax relief	Reduced tax rate	Tax holiday	Tax credit
Australia		Super deductions for R&D expenditures: deduction of up to 175% of costs			
Cambodia	Qualified investment projects: 40% additional depreciation			**Qualified investment projects: tax holiday of up to 6 years and no withholding tax on dividends**	
China		Super deductions for R&D: deduction of 150% of costs	**New/High-Technology Enterprise ("NHTE"): 15%**	**Investment of NHTE in SEZ: 2-year tax exemption followed by 3-year 50% tax reduction**	
Hong Kong	Prescribed fixed assets: immediate 100% write-off (already applicable in the base case)				
India		Infrastructure undertakings: 100% deduction of profits for a period of 10 years out of 15 or 20 years ***Special Economic Zones:*** **deduction of 100% of profits and gains in the first 5 years, 50% deduction in the subsequent 5 years**		*Development of Special Economic Zones*: exemption of income for 10 consecutive years out of any 15 years and exemption of dividend distribution tax	

(*continued*)

Table 4.1 (continued)

Territory	Reduction in taxable income		Reduction in the tax rate	Reduction in the tax liability	
	Tax deferral	Tax relief	Reduced tax rate	Tax holiday	Tax credit
		and subject to conditions a deduction of 50% for further 5 years Knowledge based sectors: deduction of 150% of expenditure incurred			
Indonesia	Eligible companies: accelerated depreciation at twice the regular rate Extended loss-carry forward of up to 10 years	**Eligible companies: reduction in net taxable income of up to 30% of the invested capital, prorated at 5% for 6 years**	Eligible companies: 50% tax rate cut in land and building tax for 8 years Eligible companies: withholding tax rate is reduced to 10%		
Japan	Initial or accelerated depreciation				Tax credit of 10% of R&D expenses
Malaysia		Companies with qualifying expenditure: double deduction of expenses		**Pioneer Status: exemption of up to 100% of statutory income for a period of up to 10 years** Investment tax allowance/re-investment allowance: tax exemption of up to 100% of statutory income depending on the amount of qualifying capital expenditure	

Philippines		Additional deduction of 50% of the wages for qualified employees for 5 years	*Special Economic Zone*: 5% tax rate on gross income	**Tax exemption for 6 years in case of pioneer firms and 4 years for non-pioneer firms**	Tax credit for taxes and duties on supplies, raw materials, and spare parts
Russia	***Special Economic Zones:* accelerated depreciation at double rates**	150% deduction of R&D expenses for certain types of research		*Special Economic Zones*: tax exemption for corporate property and land tax; some zones offer a tax holiday of up to 6 years followed by a reduced corporation tax rate	Investment tax credits of up to 30% for 1–5 years
Singapore		Qualifying companies: investment allowance of up to 100% (mostly 30%) of capital expenditure in addition to the ordinary capital allowance. Indefinite carry forward of excess allowance	Development and Expansion Incentive: concessionary tax rate of at least 5% on incremental income	**Pioneer Status: tax holiday of 5–15 years**	
		200% special tax deduction on qualifying R&D expenditure	Global Trader program: 5 or 10% concessionary tax rate on qualifying activities		
South Korea				**High-technology businesses/Foreign Investment Zones: exemption from corporation tax for 5 years and a 50% reduced tax rate for the following 2 years**	

(*continued*)

Table 4.1 (continued)

Territory	Reduction in taxable income		Reduction in the tax rate	Reduction in the tax liability	
	Tax deferral	Tax relief	Reduced tax rate	Tax holiday	Tax credit
				Free Economic Zones/ Foreign Trade Zones: 3-year tax exemption and a reduction of 50% of the tax rate for the following 2 years	
Taiwan	Machinery used for R&D purposes: service life for tax purposes is accelerated to 2 years				Investments in human resource training and R&D: tax credit of 35% of the invested amount. Credit carry forward: 5 years
Thailand	After the tax holiday, losses can be carried forward for another 5 years	*Zone 3*: double deduction for expenses on transportation, electricity and water for 10 years		**Tax exemption between 3 and 8 years for investment in certain zones; can be followed by a 50% reduced corporate tax rate for up to 5 years**	
	Initial depreciation of 40% of the cost incurred on machinery for R&D			Prioritized projects are granted an 8-year tax holiday Dividends/royalties from promoted projects are tax exempt	
Vietnam	Designated projects: accelerated depreciation at up to twice the ordinary rate		**Qualifying Companies: preferential tax rate of 10/20% applies for 15/10 years**	**Investments in designated sectors and areas: up to 4-year tax exemption and 50% reduction for the subsequent 2–9 years**	

includes for example commercial activity, tourist services, tobacco industry, real estate development, financial services, value added services in telecommunications and several more. Moreover, the invested funds must exceed certain minimum thresholds that vary according to the field of investment. Dividends paid out of such investments are tax exempt.

A tax holiday of 6 years combined with an exemption from withholding tax on dividends is calculated.

4.1.3 China

Effective from 1 January 2008, the new People's Republic of China Corporation Tax Act abolished the preferential treatment of foreign investment enterprises and foreign enterprises.[1] Instead, new tax incentives were introduced that, irrespective of the nationality of the company's shareholders, mainly encourage investments in New/High Technology Enterprises ("NHTE"), research and development activities, special economic zones ("SEZ") and special industries (e.g. specific agricultural activities, software industry, key public infrastructure, environmental protection). The Chinese tax incentive policy is primarily based on reductions in the tax rate and includes reduced tax rates as well as tax holidays.

Companies that qualify as NHTE are taxed at a reduced rate of 15% compared to the regular corporation tax rate of 25%. The main prerequisites to qualify for the tax reduction are:

- The company must have been registered in China for more than 1 year and the property rights on the core intellectual property must be located in China.
- The products of the company must fall within the scope of encouraged activities. More than 60% of the total turnover must stem from the sale of new/high technology products.
- The company must have an important share of research and development expenses that ranges between 3 and 6% of the total revenue.

Other requirements include the number of technicians involved in R&D with regard to the total number of employees, the number of employees with a university degree, the growth rate of sales and assets, etc. Detailed information is provided under the "Guidelines for the Administration of the Classification of New/High Technology Enterprises" issued by the Ministry of Science and Technology and the Ministry of Finance.

Tax holidays are granted to NHTE located in the special economic zones, to certain infrastructure or environmental protection projects as well as to software and integrated circuit production enterprises. The tax holidays provide tax exemption for 2 years in case of NHTE in special economic zones or software enterprises

[1]Grandfathering rules apply for corporations which were granted tax incentives under the Income Tax Act for Foreign Investment Enterprises and Foreign Enterprises.

and a tax exemption for 3 years in case of the eligible infrastructure or environmental protection projects. The tax holiday starts in the first income-generating year and is followed by a period of a 50% tax rate reduction that lasts 3 years. To be eligible for the tax holidays, the companies have to fulfil several requirements.

For all companies, the taxable income is reduced by means of a tax relief, if research and development costs are incurred that fulfil the requirements for a 150% super deduction.

A tax holiday of 2 years followed by a 50% reduction of corporation tax and a reduced corporation tax rate of 15% is calculated in the model.

4.1.4 Hong Kong

In Hong Kong, expenses for plant and machinery which are specifically designated to manufacturing may be written off immediately. This is conceived as a special tax incentive for investment in high-value manufacturing businesses. Furthermore, patents and other intangibles are not capitalised and depreciated over their useful lives either, but are written off to expense as incurred. Both regulations have already been implemented for the base case scenario, since a manufacturing corporation is assumed. Therefore, no additional incentives are considered in this chapter.

4.1.5 India

With the aim view of promoting the development of infrastructure and the industrialisation of certain areas, the Indian government offers several tax incentives. A 100% deduction of profits out of infrastructure undertakings is available for 10 years out of 15 years (20 years in some cases). To encourage the development of Special Economic Zones, a tax exemption is granted on income derived by companies developing these zones. The tax exemption lasts for ten consecutive years out of any 15 years beginning from the year in which the SEZ is notified. In addition, such companies are exempt from dividend distribution tax. Newly established companies in Special Economic Zones (SEZ) may qualify for a 100% deduction of profits in the first 5 years followed by a 50% deduction for the subsequent 5 years and possibly a 50% deduction for another 5 years.

With regard to tax incentives for investments in R&D activities, qualifying expenditure can be deducted at 150% of the invested amount. Several other incentives will no longer be granted after the financial year ending in 2009. This concerns, among other regulations, export related incentives and undertakings in free trade zones.

A deduction of 100% of profits and gains in the first 5 years followed by a 50% deduction in the subsequent 10 years is used for calculations.

4.1.6 Indonesia

Companies investing in certain sectors and/or regions qualify for tax incentives under Indonesian tax law. Designated economic activities include the food industry, pharmaceuticals, iron and steel, machinery and equipment, and industrial chemicals. The Indonesian tax authorities grant a tax relief equal to 30% of the invested capital. This allowance can be claimed as a deduction from the taxable income and must be prorated at 5% for 6 years provided that the assets invested are not transferred within this time. The taxable income may also be reduced by accelerated depreciation. The applicable depreciation rate is twice the ordinary rate. In case of loss-making companies that qualify for tax incentives, an extended loss-carry forward of up to 10 years is granted. As for land and building tax, qualifying companies are eligible to a 50% tax rate cut for the first 8 years under the condition that the investment is new and takes place in one of the encouraged provinces and sectors. The encouraged sectors include for example the food industry, garments and textiles, pharmaceuticals, machinery and equipment, electronics. Moreover, concerning cross-border transactions, the withholding tax rate on dividends is reduced to from 20 to 10%, unless a lower rate applies under a tax treaty which is the case for the locations of parent companies considered in this study.

A reduction in net taxable income of 30%, prorated at 5% over 6 years is implemented into the model.

4.1.7 Japan

Taxpayers can file a claim to use the higher of initial or accelerated depreciation in the first year or in subsequent years.

A tax credit against corporation tax is granted for R&D expenditures. It is calculated as 10% of all R&D expenses plus 5% of the increased R&D expenditure compared to the average of the past 3 years. Small- and medium-sized companies are granted a 12% tax credit.

Since no more information on the initial and accelerated depreciation was available and R&D incentives cannot be implemented, no incentive is calculated for Japan.

4.1.8 Malaysia

The tax incentives available in Malaysia are manifold. The extent of exemption under each type of tax incentive varies. Companies with Pioneer status enjoy a tax exemption of up to 100% of their statutory income for a period of up to 10 years. Investments receiving preferential treatment under the Pioneer status are usually of national and strategic importance, located in certain underdeveloped areas or are based on intensive R&D or high technology activities.

Under the investment tax allowance, companies are eligible to deduct a percentage of qualifying capital expenditure (between 50 and 100%) from a certain percentage of statutory income (between 70 and 100%) for 5–10 years. The allowance is only granted in the year of expenditure, but an excess amount can be carried forward up to 10 years. Qualifying expenditures include expenses for R&D companies, high technology companies or for investments located in promoted areas.

A reinvestment allowance is given to companies investing in a factory, plant or machinery used for qualifying projects. Sixty percent of capital expenditure can then be set off against 70–100% of statutory income for 15 consecutive years. Qualifying projects include expanding, modernising or automating an existing business.

For all allowances, it is true that dividends paid out of exempt income are also exempt from tax in the hands of the recipient.

Double deductions or special deductions are available for certain companies with qualifying expenditures. Moreover numerous sector specific incentives are granted. With regard to the encouragement of foreign direct investment, the Malaysian government is trying to attract foreign investors by pre-package incentives. These pre-package incentives are conceived as a kind of "wish list" of the foreign investor for tax incentives. When granting these company-specific incentives, factors such as size of investment, level of spin-off, employment opportunities, technology transfer, and national and strategic importance are considered.

An exemption of 100% of statutory income for 10 years is used for calculations.

4.1.9 Philippines

In order to be eligible for tax incentives, investors must be registered with the Board of Investments (BOI) which is subject to certain conditions. If the applying corporation is not more than 60% owned by Filipino nationals the investor has to engage in qualified projects listed by the BOI in the Investment Priorities Plan (IPP). If registered, new pioneer firms are granted a 6-year tax exemption, whereas new non-pioneer firms are granted a 4-year exemption. The exemption may be extended under certain conditions. A pioneer enterprise is engaged in the manufacturing, processing or production of goods, products or other materials that are not usually produced on the Philippines or that use an entirely different design, formula or process of production. An additional deduction of 50% for labour costs is available in the first 5 years from registration for skilled and unskilled labour workers. The deduction is not granted in addition to a tax holiday. A tax credit is given for taxes and duties on supplies, raw materials, and spare parts used for the manufacturing of products that will later be exported.

In Special Economic Zones (SEZ) no taxes are imposed other than a 5% tax on gross income. Three percent of this goes to the national government and 2% to the local government. Companies can be located in a SEZ and in addition registered with the BOI. They can then use the tax holiday and afterwards the 5% tax rate.

A tax exemption of 6 years is calculated in the model.

4.1.10 Russia

If a company develops new equipment, new technology or creates new kinds of raw and other materials, or contributes significantly to the socio-economic development of a region, an investment tax credit of up to 30% is granted. The amount is fixed by agreement and is in general granted for 1–5 years.

Companies in Special Economic Zones (SEZ) are eligible for accelerated depreciation at double rates. They are also exempt from corporate property tax and land tax. Some SEZs also offer tax holidays of up to 6 years followed by a reduced corporation tax rate.

R&D expenses for certain types of research, just as medical, nuclear technology or cell technology, can be deducted at 150%.

An accelerated depreciation at double rates is implemented into the model.

4.1.11 Singapore

Singapore offers a wide range of investment tax incentives. As regards general tax incentives, they are in most cases conceived as reductions in the tax rate either by means of tax holidays or by special reduced rates that are applied on qualifying parts of the corporate income. A tax holiday is available for companies that qualify for the pioneer status. A pioneer status is granted based on the level of investment, skills and technology, the beneficial effect on Singapore and the product produced. The minimum period of tax exemption is 5 years and the maximum 15 years. Dividends paid out of exempt income by a pioneer company are tax free in the hand of the recipient. Companies engaging in high value-added activities that are expanded and upgraded in Singapore are eligible to a special tax rate of at least 5% on the incremental income (Development and Expansion Incentive).

Global trading companies establishing their regional or global offshore trading base in Singapore enjoy reduced rates of 5 or 10% on qualifying activities. Apart from the incentives for qualifying investors, Singapore also offers incentives for certain projects. These include for instance a capital allowance of up to 100% of the amount of capital invested. In most cases, the capital allowance is 30%. The allowance reduced the capital income in addition to ordinary depreciation allowances. If the allowance exceeds the taxable income of one period, it can be carried forward indefinitely. Approved R&D projects are granted a tax deduction of up to 200% on qualifying R&D expenditure.

A tax holiday of 15 years is implemented into the model.

4.1.12 South Korea

In 1998, Korea has established the Foreign Investment Promotion Act (FIPA) which is supposed to attract mainly high-technology and large-scale manufacturing investment by granting partial and full exemption on corporate income tax. The foreign investor must hold at least 10% of outstanding shares of the foreign invested company or the corporation must be located in a Foreign Investment Zone (FIZ). High-technology businesses are then granted a 5-year tax exemption followed by a 2-year reduction of 50% of the tax rate. Foreign investors can use a Tax Exemption and Reduction Checking System which allows them to determine their tax benefit eligibility before making commitments in Korea. The benefit is substantially less when acquiring an existing firm (50% exemption for the first 3 years and 30% exemption for the following 2 years). An FIZ can be established for investments in manufacturing which exceed $50 million or a certain number of employees or large-scale investments in tourism. Dividends paid by companies that benefit from tax exemption are granted the same benefits.

Free Trade Zones aim to attract manufacturing, trade, logistics and distribution by exempting or reducing customs duties and taxes. Free Economic Zones are designated areas and try to offer an optimal business and living environment by offering resources and amenities for international communities and attracting investments by reducing taxes or granting a tax holiday. In both zones, the share of profits that equals the share of foreign investors in the company, is eligible for a tax exemption of 3 years followed by a 50% tax rate reduction for the two subsequent years.

A tax exemption of 5 years followed by a 50% reduction of corporation tax rate for 2 years is used for the calculations.

4.1.13 Taiwan

From 1 January 1991 to 31 December 2009, tax incentives in Taiwan were regulated by the Statute for Industrial Upgrading. Under this act, emerging or strategic enterprises are granted a 5-year tax holiday. To encourage investments in production automation or information technology a tax credit of up to 20% was provided. Yet, both measures will no longer be available under the Industrial Innovation Act which will replace the Statute for Industrial Upgrading in 2010. A special focus of the new act is on research and development, human resources training, operations headquarters and international logistics and distribution centres. Therefore, a tax credit for human resource training and R&D activities will presumably persist under the new act. The tax credit amounts to 35% of the funds invested. Any excess credit can be carried forward for 5 years. If the expenses in R&D activities increased within the last 2 years, an additional tax credit of 50% of the incremental amount is granted. The depreciation of machinery which is exclusively used for R&D purposes may be accelerated to 2 years.

Since only incentives for R&D activities are granted, no incentive is calculated in the model.

4.1.14 Thailand

For investments in qualifying zones (Zone 1–3), Thailand grants a tax holiday between 3 and 8 years. The underlying project has to fulfil certain requirements; otherwise, the tax holiday can be nullified afterwards. Dividends paid out of exempt profits are also exempt from taxes (including withholding taxes). If losses occur during the tax holiday, they can be carried forward another 5 years after the end of the tax holiday. In Zone 3, the corporation tax rate can be reduced by 50% for 5 years after the tax holiday. Also, a double deduction of expenses on transportation, electricity and water supply is possible for 10 years in Zone 3.

Royalties paid from a promoted project are exempt from corporate tax within 5 years from the day the project starts to earn profits. Promoted projects are registered by the Board of Investments (BOI) on a project to project basis.

Expenses for machinery bought for R&D purposes can be deducted by an initial depreciation of 40% in the year of acquisition.

Prioritised projects are granted a tax holiday for 8 years, regardless of their location. Such projects include activities related directly to the development of technology and human resources or activities related to targeted industries.

A tax exemption of 8 years followed by a 50% tax rate reduction for 5 years is implemented into the model.

4.1.15 Vietnam

According to the sector of investment and the geographical area, Vietnam provides several tax incentives which are mainly conceived as reductions in the tax rate. Apart from supporting investments in high technology and scientific research, an important focus of the Vietnamese tax incentives is on the encouragement of areas with difficult or especially difficult socio-economic conditions. A preferential tax rate of 10% for a period of 15 years is available for the following companies:

- Companies newly set up in locations with especially difficult socioeconomic conditions
- Companies newly set up in economic zones or high technology zones
- Newly set up companies investing in high technology projects, scientific research and technological developments
- Newly set up companies investing in designated sectors such as for example manufacture of composite materials, production of high quality steel, production of medical equipment for analytical purposes, production of medicine adopting advanced technology or biotechnology, production of computers

Companies newly set up in areas with difficult socioeconomic conditions are eligible to a reduced rate of 20% for a period of 10 years.

Companies qualifying for preferential tax rates may also be entitled to tax holidays. According to the characteristics of the investment, the tax exemption may be up to 4 years and is followed by a period of 50% tax rate reduction that lasts between 2 and 9 years. Tax exemption is also available for predefined types of income that are for instance derived from projects related to scientific research and technological development (exemption limited to 1 year), from projects related to certain fields of agriculture or from training projects for ethnic minorities or disabled people.

Moreover, an accelerated depreciation is available for companies yielding a high economic efficiency and operating in investment incentive sectors and designated regions. The depreciation rate for accelerated depreciation cannot exceed twice the ordinary rate.

A tax exemption of 4 years followed by a 50% rate reduction for 9 years, combined with a reduced corporation tax rate of 10% for 15 years is used for calculations.

4.2 Impact on the Tax Burdens at the Level of the Subsidiary

The tax incentives have a significant impact on the level of the effective tax burden and on the ranking of the territories in this study. For each territory, the following calculations are based on the tax incentives marked in Table 4.1. The chosen measures have been classified as a typical incentive in the respective territories. Figure 4.1 displays the impact of the selected tax incentives on the EATR at the subsidiary level. To quantify the impact of tax incentives, our model outlined in Chap. 3 is based on a going-concern assumption. This means that only the net present value of a tax incentive is taken into account. For example, a tax holiday for a certain number of years does not reduce the effective tax rate to zero indefinitely because profits are subject to taxation after the tax relief has expired.

The cases where profits are exempt from tax show the highest reduction in tax burden. It can especially be seen that the longer the period of exemption, the stronger the relief (e.g. tax holiday of 15 years in Singapore). The indefinite reduced tax rate in China, from 25 to 15% for qualified high technology projects, also shows a high impact on the effective tax burden. In India, the 50% reduction of the tax rate for 10 years, after a 5-year tax exemption, accounts for a high portion of tax reduction since the combined corporate tax rate on profits in India is rather high. The figure also shows that in territories where the effective average tax rate is relatively low compared to the general tax rate on profits, the effect of a tax holiday is higher than in territories where the effective average tax rate is high. The reason is that the higher the effective average tax rate in relation to the tax rate on profits, the higher is the burden from non-income taxes. Such taxes are usually not affected by tax holidays that is why their impact does not change due to the tax incentive.

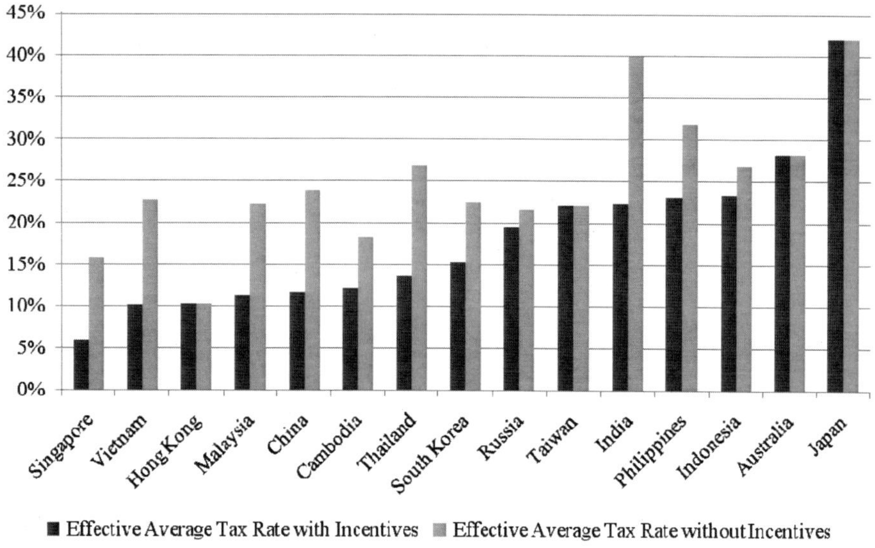

Fig. 4.1 Impact of tax incentives on domestic investment; see Table A.5

Accelerated or additional depreciation is only modelled for two countries (Indonesia and Russia). The figure shows that such incentives have the least impact on the tax burden. They can only reduce the effective average tax rate by 2–4% points.

The ranking of territories has changed including tax incentives. Vietnam has become the country with the second smallest tax burden while without incentives it was ranked average. In comparison, Russia and Taiwan became less attractive since they offer no or only minor tax incentives. Since for Japan no tax incentives are considered in the calculations, it remains a high-tax country while India can reduce its tax burden by almost one half, but still is an investment location with a relatively high tax burden.

Overall it can be shown that tax incentives in the Asia-Pacific region offer high reductions in tax burden, e.g. up to about 60% in the case of Singapore. This shows that the territories considered are highly interested in supporting foreign direct investment or generally investment in certain projects or regions. But it has to be kept in mind that the calculated incentives have different prerequisites, therefore different types of investment are examined in this chapter.

4.3 Impact on the Tax Burdens at the Level of the German and the US Parent Company

From the perspective of a multinational investor, i.e. a German or US parent company, the tax incentives have a considerable impact on the ranking of the territories from the highest to the lowest EATR. Because profits from foreign

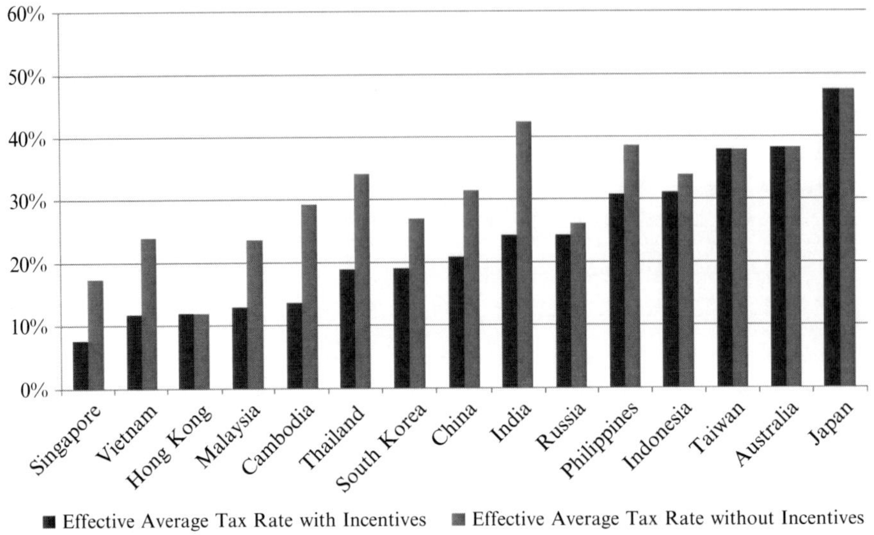

Fig. 4.2 Impact of tax incentives on German outbound investments to the Asia-Pacific region, India, and Russia; see Table A.6

investments (i.e. dividends) are 95% exempt from taxation in Germany, a German parent company also benefits from the incentives if the profits are transferred to Germany. In contrast, in the US, foreign profits are not exempt, but foreign tax is credited against US taxes. Therefore, a lower taxation due to incentives may not be transferred to the parent company if US taxes exceed the level of foreign taxes. Profits are then taxed at the higher US tax rate. Figure 4.2 displays the impact of the selected tax incentives on the EATR at the level of the German parent company.

In Cambodia, where the withholding tax is reduced to zero for qualifying projects, the impact on the overall tax burden is large, since the taxation compared to the domestic case is only increased by the taxation of 5% of the dividends. In Singapore, a significant impact can also be described. Due to a 15-year tax holiday and a withholding tax of 0%, the tax burden for the German parent company can be reduced to 7.5%. Overall, the effects are similar to the results of the domestic case, only where withholding taxes are reduced (i.e. Cambodia, South Korea, and Thailand) in addition to the tax incentive on local profits, the impact is larger (Table 4.2).

For Australia, Japan, and Taiwan no tax incentives are considered. It can be seen that those territories are ranked 13th, 14th and 15th applying tax incentives. The tax incentive in Hong Kong is already applicable in the base case and no additional tax incentives apply, but since the tax burden is already relatively low without incentives, it is still ranked third. Singapore decreases its tax burden by more than half through tax incentives and is then ranked as the territory with the lowest EATR. Thailand and India both offer attractive tax incentives which allow them to advance by four and five positions in the ranking respectively. Although Russia offers an accelerated depreciation, it loses four ranking positions because the offered tax

Table 4.2 Impact of tax incentives on German outbound investment to the Asia-Pacific region, India, and Russia

Territory	Without tax incentives		With tax incentives	
	EATR (%)	Ranking	EATR (%)	Ranking
Australia	38.4	12	38.4	14
Cambodia	29.3	7	13.6	5
China	31.5	8	20.7	8
Hong Kong	11.8	1	11.8	3
India	42.5	14	24.3	9
Indonesia	34.1	9	31.1	12
Japan	47.7	15	47.7	15
Malaysia	23.7	3	12.7	4
Philippines	38.7	13	30.8	11
Russia	26.3	5	24.4	10
Singapore	17.3	2	7.5	1
South Korea	27.1	6	19.1	7
Taiwan	37.9	11	37.9	13
Thailand	34.2	10	18.9	6
Vietnam	24.1	4	11.7	2

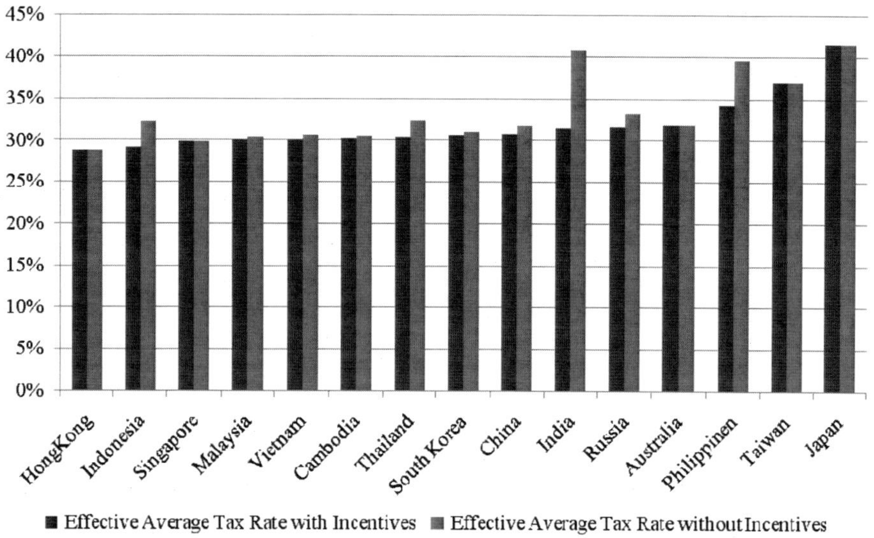

Fig. 4.3 Impact of tax incentives on US outbound investment to the Asia-Pacific region, India, and Russia; see Table A.7

incentive has a relatively low impact on the tax burden compared to the in most cases offered tax holiday.

Figure 4.3 shows the impact of the selected tax incentives on the EATR at the level of the US parent company. The results show that the consequences of using tax incentives for a US parent company are, because of the credit method for avoiding double taxation, not very large. Only India shows a significant effect because the tax burden without incentives is at about 41% and thereby higher than the tax burden in the US (about 35%). The foreign taxes paid then result in an excess credit. The relatively attractive incentives in India cause the tax burden to go down by almost one half in the domestic case. Therefore in the cross-border case no excess credit results and tax burden goes down significantly. It has to be pointed out that a valid tax strategy in a country applying the credit method is to retain profits in the territory of the subsidiary for several periods. This results in a significant reduction of tax burden since taxation can be postponed to later periods in time. But as only a profit retention of one period can be implemented in the model, the results of such a tax strategy cannot be shown.

If the country of the parent company offers the credit method, it can be seen that the tax burden for each territory of the subsidiary is rather similar. The low taxation for example in Hong Kong and Singapore cannot be transferred to the parent company. Therefore, the application of tax incentives does not result in a significant tax burden reduction. It can be said that the taxation of the foreign profits is raised to the level of the US parent company, non-income taxation then adds upon that. Therefore, territories where profits taxation is decreased by tax incentives, but non-income taxation is still prevalent, have a relatively high tax burden overall. For example, Hong Kong is ranked first with and without incentives although the domestic tax burden is higher than in the case of Singapore and the withholding tax in both cases is 0%. That shows that the non-income taxation in Singapore outweighs the advantage of the low profits taxation (Table 4.3).

Comparing the results for the German and the US parent company, the differences between the exemption and credit system of avoiding double taxation, become obvious. As in the case of Germany, tax incentives lead to a significantly lower tax burden, which is not the case for the US parent which is also due to the

Table 4.3 Impact of tax incentives on US outbound investment to the Asia-Pacific region, India, and Russia

Territory	Without tax incentives		With tax incentives	
	EATR (%)	Ranking	EATR (%)	Ranking
Australia	31.9	8	31.9	12
Cambodia	30.6	4	30.2	6
China	31.7	7	30.8	9
Hong Kong	28.8	1	28.8	1
India	40,9	14	31.5	10
Indonesia	32.2	9	29.2	2
Japan	41.6	15	41.6	15
Malaysia	30.3	3	29.9	4
Philippines	39.6	13	34.2	13
Russia	33.3	11	31.6	11
Singapore	29.9	2	29.9	2
South Korea	31.1	6	30.7	8
Taiwan	37.0	12	37.0	14
Thailand	32.3	10	30.3	7
Vietnam	30.7	5	30.0	5

limitations of the model. For Asian territories trying to attract foreign direct investment that means that investors coming from credit countries might not be as affected by tax incentives as investors from countries practicing the exemption method.

4.4 Tax Incentives for Group Structures

Several territories in the Asia-Pacific region offer tax incentives especially aimed at attracting headquarters and holding companies. The establishment of such offices has several positive effects on the selected territory. Not only do the names of big companies attract other investors and make locations more appealing. Also, employees of such headquarters are usually well educated which leads to highly paid workers living in the area (see Testa et al. (2005) and Katz (2002)). In addition, headquarters are in need of business services providers which they will possibly acquire locally. All these factors make the allocation of headquarters so interesting. Out of the territories considered, Australia, Malaysia, the Philippines, Singapore, Taiwan, and Thailand grant incentives especially for headquarters or holding companies. These incentives will be presented in this chapter, but will not be quantified in the model. Table 4.4 provides an overview of the tax incentives.

In *Australia*, regional headquarters are allowed to immediately deduct set-up costs incurred within 12 months before or after the date the headquarters first derives assessable income. Costs of tangible assets may not be deducted.

An approved Operational Headquarters (OHQ) in *Malaysia* is exempt from tax for 10 years on the following income:

- Income from services provided to its offices or related companies outside Malaysia.
- Income from services provided to its offices or related companies in Malaysia, provided such income does not exceed 20% of the income from qualifying services.
- Interest on foreign currency loans extended to its offices or related companies outside Malaysia.
- Royalties received from research and development work carried out in Malaysia on behalf of its offices or related companies outside Malaysia.

An approved operational headquarters (OHQ) is a locally incorporated company that carries on a business in Malaysia to provide qualifying services to its offices or related companies within or outside Malaysia.

In Malaysia, a representative office and regional office of a foreign corporation engaging in the manufacturing and trading sector is an office that is established to perform certain activities which are not profit-making. Therefore, such offices are exempt from tax.

An Investment Holding Company in Malaysia, conducting only activities which consist of making investments, is allowed to deduct certain expenses from aggregate income which are normally not deductible. Permitted expenses include director's

Table 4.4 Summary of tax incentives for group structures in the Asia-Pacific region, India, and Russia

Territory	Reduction in taxable income		Reduction in the tax rate	Reduction in the tax liability	
	Tax deferral	Tax relief	Reduced tax rate	Tax holiday	Tax credit
Australia	*Regional Headquarters*: immediate deduction of set-up costs				
Malaysia		*Investment Holding Company*: deduction of qualifying expenses		*Operational Headquarters*: 10-year tax exemption for certain types of income *Representative/regional office*: tax exemption of certain types of income	
Philippines			*Regional Operating Headquarters*: corporation tax of 10% on net taxable income	*Regional/Area Headquarters*: tax exemption	
Singapore			*Headquarters Awards*: reduced tax rate of 15% for 3 years (regional HQ) or 0–10% for 5–20 years (international HQ) *Operational Headquarters*: qualifying income is subject to a 10% reduced tax rate	*Operational Headquarters*: dividend income is tax exempt	
Taiwan				*Operation Headquarters*: tax exemption of qualifying income	
Thailand			*Regional Operating Headquarters*: reduced corporate tax rate of 10% on qualifying income		

fees, wages, salaries and allowances, management fees, secretarial, audit and accounting fees, telephone charges, printing, stationery costs and postage, and rent and other expenses incidental to the maintenance office. The deduction is limited to 5% of gross income from dividends, interest and rent. Expenses that cannot be fully deducted in a year, due to a loss or insufficient aggregate income, cannot be carried forward to subsequent years.

Where an Investment Holding Company is listed on Bursa Malaysia, the income from the holding of investments is treated as gross income from a business source of that Investment Holding Company. Expenses incurred by the Investment Holding Company are accorded full deduction. Unutilised losses and unabsorbed capital allowances cannot be carried forward.

On the *Philippines*, regional or area headquarters of multinational companies – used to coordinate affiliates, subsidiaries or branches in the Asia-Pacific region – are exempt from income tax. Regionally operating headquarters only pay 10% tax on their net taxable income. An operating headquarter is usually a branch of a multinational firm that provides qualifying services just as administration, research or marketing, to its affiliates, subsidiaries or branches in the Asia-Pacific region.

Singapore intends to increase the number of headquarters located in the territory and therefore offers reduced tax rates on incremental qualifying income. The rate amounts to 15% for regional headquarters and 0, 5 or 10% for international headquarters. This kind of preferential treatment is limited to 3 years for regional headquarters and 5–20 years for international headquarters. The Headquarters Programme is applicable to Singaporean entities which provide holding company activities to their related companies worldwide.

If a holding company receives exempt dividends from its wholly owned pioneer subsidiary, it may pass them to its own shareholders who are again tax exempt.

Operational headquarters are offered several incentives in Singapore. Management fee income, other headquarters-related income, and interest and royalty income is subject to a 10% reduced tax for up to 10 years. Dividend income is tax exempt for 10 years. An operational headquarters is an entity located in Singapore for the purpose of providing management and other related services to subsidiaries in other countries.

If an operation headquarters in *Taiwan* reaches a certain size and accrues economic benefits, qualifying types of income are tax exempt. Such income includes income from the provision of management services or research and development services to its affiliates abroad, royalty payments received from its affiliates abroad and investment returns and profits from the disposal of assets received from investments in its affiliates abroad.

Regional Operating Headquarters (ROH) in *Thailand* are, under certain conditions, granted a reduced corporate tax rate of 10% on certain income which includes interest income from loans and royalties for R&D. The most important conditions are that the ROH carries out services for affiliates in at least three foreign countries and that the income from such services must exceed 50% of aggregate income.

Hong Kong does not have any special tax incentive for headquarters, but Hong Kong exercises a source-based taxation, meaning that only profits which have their source in Hong Kong are taxed. Profits arising from services done for related companies outside of Hong Kong are generally considered to have their source outside Hong Kong and are therefore not taxed. For those reasons, Hong Kong is a location of a great number of regional headquarters.

Overall, it can be said that tax incentives for headquarters are partly very generous. Territories like Hong Kong, the Philippines, Malaysia, and Taiwan even offer an indefinite tax exemption for qualifying income. But it is important to note that not only low taxation causes multinational companies to establish their headquarters in a certain territory. Other important factors are a free flow of information, the absence of exchange controls, a corruption free government or political stability and security (see Census and Statistics Department (2008)).

Chapter 5
Tax Planning Strategies

The East-Asian market has become increasingly interesting in the past years for investors from Europe and the United States. Direct investment from Germany to the fifteen territories has almost increased tenfold within the last 15 years (see Deutsche Bundesbank (1989–2007)). For the United States, the numbers show a similar trend as investments are six times as high as they were as 15 years ago (see Bureau of Economic Analyses (1989–2007)). One reason certainly is the exploitation of Asian-Pacific markets which amount to one third of worldwide GDP.

Since tax policies play a great role in choosing a location for investment, tax planning strategies for multinationals have to be considered for investments in the Asia-Pacific region. The main interest of a parent company is to face a low tax burden on foreign profits and on their repatriation. Instruments to achieve such objectives are for example the location decision, the decision of financing and the establishment of holding structures. The first two topics have been covered in Chap. 3 of this study and will not be examined in great detail in this chapter.

Since tax planning strategies differ between countries using the exemption or the credit method in order to avoid double taxation, they have to be developed separately in the cases of Germany and the United States. Strategies for German multinationals will first be looked at, followed by strategies for US multinationals. The underlying structure for the investment is shown in Fig. 5.1.

5.1 German Parent Company

In this simple example, it is assumed that the parent company is interested in receiving foreign profits either in the form of dividends or in the form of interest. For this chapter, the location decision is already made and the goal is to reduce the tax burden for the investment at the specified location.[1]

[1]For favourable locations for subsidiaries see Chap. 3.

D. Endres et al. (eds.), *Company Taxation in the Asia-Pacific Region, India, and Russia*, DOI 10.1007/978-3-642-12217-0_5, © Springer-Verlag Berlin Heidelberg 2010

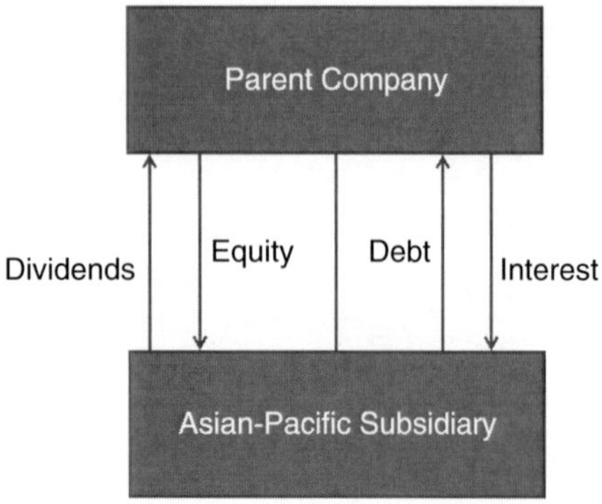

Fig. 5.1 Basic structure of investment

Table 5.1 Withholding tax rates on dividends

Territory	Withholding tax on dividends (%)
Australia	15
Cambodia	14
China	10
Hong Kong	**0**
India	**0**
Indonesia	10
Japan	10
Malaysia	**0**
Philippines	10
Russia	5
Singapore	**0**
South Korea	5
Taiwan	20
Thailand	10
Vietnam	**0**

As Germany uses the exemption method for repatriated profits, the withholding tax on dividends plays a great role for tax planning. This tax is levied on dividends at source and cannot be credited against German corporation tax as dividends lead to tax-exempt income. It therefore becomes a definite tax burden on foreign profits. Table 5.1 shows withholding tax rates for dividends in the considered territories.

Hong Kong, India, Malaysia, Singapore, and Vietnam show a very attractive withholding tax rate of 0%. In the case of India, it has to be pointed out that a dividend distribution tax of 17% is levied on repatriated profits. Therefore, the low withholding tax is outweighed by the high tax burden on distributed profits (see also Chap. 3).

By setting up a holding structure, such withholding tax rates may be reduced or even avoided if double tax treaties between the countries considered offer lower rates than German tax treaties. But it has to be kept in mind that an additional tax burden on the level of the holding company may occur. Thus, in order to benefit from a holding structure, the overall tax burden must be lower than in the case of a direct participation. Therefore the positive and negative effects have to be judged as a whole and potentially advantageous structures identified.

Table A.8 shows withholding tax rates on dividends between all considered territories. The comparison with withholding taxes paid for a direct repatriation to Germany reveals that several advantageous combinations exist, where the withholding tax burden may be reduced. Several examples are shown in Fig. 5.2.

The figure shows that the establishment of a holding company may decrease the withholding tax burden. In the case of a Chinese, Japanese or Australian subsidiary, the tax burden can be reduced by 5% points, for a Taiwanese subsidiary, even a reduction of 7.5% points is possible. But in order to judge the overall effect, it is important to know how received dividends are taxed in the territory of the holding company. If a credit system exists, dividends are taxed at the according corporate tax rate and withholding tax rate is credited against such tax. This leads to an increase of the overall tax burden since national corporate tax rates are in all cases higher than withholding tax rates. Therefore, a holding structure is only reasonable when foreign dividends from a substantial holding are exempt in the holding company domicile. For the territories shown in Fig. 5.2, this is the case for Hong Kong, Malaysia, Russia, and Singapore. Implementing a holding structure using those territories as the holding company domicile can be very attractive for German parent companies. If all profits are distributed to the parent, a decrease of 5% points of the withholding tax rate can lead to a substantial reduction of the overall tax burden.

This result does not take into account any tax incentives offered in the considered territories, but it becomes evident that two out of the four holding company domiciles are territories also offering generous tax incentives as described in Chap. 4. Those incentives are mainly for regional or operational headquarters

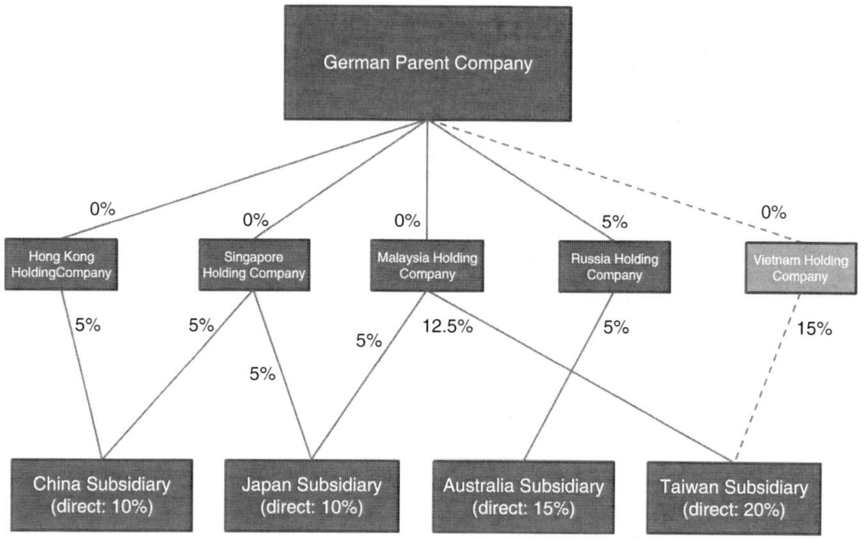

Fig. 5.2 Reduction of withholding tax by setting up holding structures

which also incur certain services for their subsidiaries. This means that even if the holding company provides services for their subsidiaries besides purely holding the participation, income may be tax exempt for a certain time period or even indefinitely. In this context, it is also apparent that territories like the Philippines, Taiwan, and Thailand, which also offer generous tax incentives, are not attractive for German investors, as their withholding tax rates are relatively high, in some cases because of an insufficient set of tax treaties. Also the German regulations for controlled foreign companies should not be neglected. Passive income of subsidiaries in low tax territories can be subject to German taxation which then results in a higher tax burden and can change the expected results.[2]

To avoid high profits taxation at the subsidiary level, the investment can be financed by debt, since interest is generally deductible from taxable income. This has been discussed in Chap. 3, but so-called thin capitalisation rules can limit the deductibility of interest payments if certain debt-to-equity ratios are exceeded or if the proportion of interest paid to related parties is too high. As Table 5.2 shows, not all Asian-Pacific territories impose such rules.

Within the limitations of these rules, interest payments can be deducted from taxable profits and are taxed in the hands of the recipient. A possibly incurring withholding tax is credited against German corporate income tax. Withholding tax rates vary between 0 and 20%, thus a credit against corporation tax should generally be possible. Only, if no other profits occur in Germany with a subsidiary located in Taiwan, levying a withholding tax rate of 20%, an excess tax credit could result as

Table 5.2 Thin capitalisation rules in the Asia-Pacific region, India, and Russia

Territory	Thin capitalisation rules
Australia	Interest is deductible up to 75% of the average net value of risk weighted Australian assets
Cambodia	–
China	Interest is deductible up to a 2:1 debt to equity ratio
Hong Kong	–
India	–
Indonesia	–
Japan	Interest is deductible up to three times the company's net equity owned by the foreign shareholder who receives the interest payments
Malaysia	Thin capitalisation rules are imposed on a case-by-case basis
Philippines	Thin capitalisation rules are imposed on a case-by-case basis
Russia	Interest is deductible up to a 3:1 debt to equity ratio
Singapore	–
South Korea	Interest is deductible up to a 3:1 debt to equity ratio
Taiwan	–
Thailand	–
Vietnam	–

[2]For more information see Jacobs (2008, pp. 471–479).

the corporation tax rate is only 15% in Germany. For this constellation, it may be reasonable to establish a holding company, in order to reduce the withholding tax burden. But Table A.9, showing all withholding tax rates on interest in the considered territories, demonstrates that there is no possible combination for the reduction of the 20% withholding tax rate within the territories.

If the high tax burden on the level of the subsidiary should still be reduced by deducting interest payments from taxable profit, interest earnings can be received by a financing company in a territory with a lower tax burden than Germany and then possibly be repatriated in the form of dividends to Germany, which in turn are tax exempt. Since interest payments are usually part of taxable income in the country of the recipient, this structure is only reasonable for financing companies with a lower tax on profits than in Germany. In order to compare the tax burden, the income tax on distributed profits has to be set in relation to the income tax in Germany, which is 30.8%.[3] Therefore, India, Japan, and the Philippines do not qualify as the recipient of interest instead of Germany because in these countries income tax rates are even higher. For all other territories, withholding taxes on dividends have to be taken into account. This leads again to the favourable implementation of dividend distribution discussed in Chap. 3 and earlier in this chapter. For the deductibility of interest payments, thin capitalisation rules have to be considered. By the discussed structure, the tax burden can be reduced significantly. This is shown in Fig. 5.3 using the example of India.

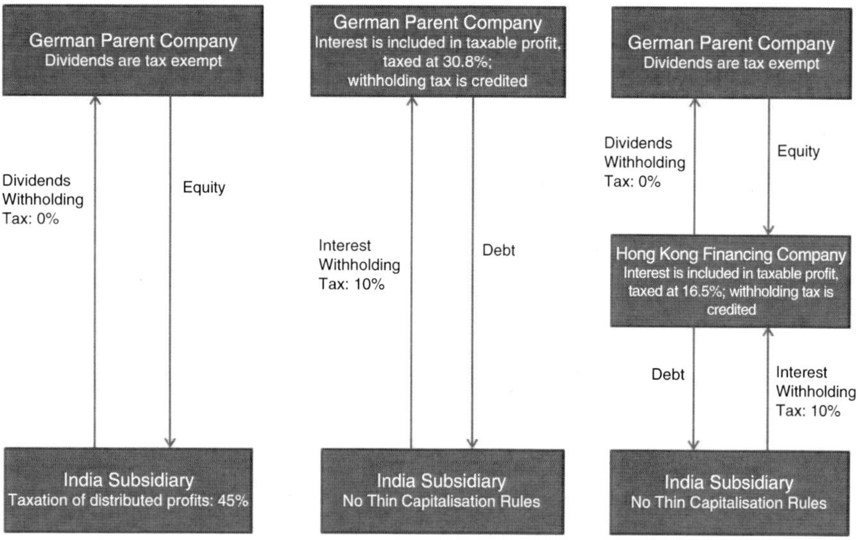

Fig. 5.3 Different financing structures

[3]Corporation tax of 15% plus solidarity surcharge of 5.5%; trade tax calculated by 3.5% × a multiplier of 428%. Combined tax rate = (0.15 + 1.055) + (0.035 × 4.28) = 30.8%.

It can be seen that in the case of equity financing, distributed profits are taxed at 45% in India. By financing with debt, the tax burden can be reduced to 30.8%, which is the income taxation of German profits. By adding a financing company in Hong Kong, the tax burden can be reduced even more. Interest is fully deductible in India and taxed in Hong Kong at a rate of only 16.5% while the underlying withholding tax of 10% can be credited. If after-tax profits are repatriated to Germany, no withholding tax is levied.

5.2 US Parent Company

In the case of US investments to the Asia-Pacific region, the same basic structure is assumed as shown in Fig. 5.1. As the United States use the credit method for repatriated profits and interest, underlying corporation tax and withholding tax will be credited against US corporate income tax. It is therefore important to ensure that no excess credit results since that leads to a definite tax burden on foreign profits. The foreign tax credit is generally limited to the US tax liability on all foreign income (overall limitation). Table 5.3 shows the creditable tax burden on dividends and on interest in the territories considered.

The corporation tax rate of US corporations is currently 38.85%,[4] but withholding taxes can only be credited against federal tax which is levied at 35%. In the case of dividends, several territories impose higher creditable taxes which lead to an excess credit. This is the case for India, Indonesia, Japan, the Philippines, Taiwan, and Thailand. But in India, Indonesia, the Philippines, and Thailand tax incentives

Table 5.3 Creditable tax burden on dividends and on interest

Territory	Creditable taxes on dividends (%)	Creditable taxes on interest (%)
Australia	30.0	10
Cambodia	31.2	14
China	32.5	10
Hong Kong	16.5	0
India	**45.2**	15
Indonesia	35.2	10
Japan	**40.8**	10
Malaysia	25.0	15
Philippines	**40.9**	15
Russia	24.0	0
Singapore	18.0	15
South Korea	31.2	12
Taiwan	**40.0**	20
Thailand	37.0	15
Vietnam	25.0	10

[4]The state profits tax of California is taken as an example.

may reduce the tax burden in which case no excess credit may result. Since an overall limitation is applied, higher creditable taxes can also be compensated by lower rates from other subsidiaries.

The creditable tax in the case of interest payments only consists of the withholding tax. It can be seen that no such rate exceeds the corporation tax rate of the US parent company. Thus, even if no other profits are generated, withholding taxes will be fully creditable. A further reduction of withholding taxes does not result in a lower tax burden since foreign repatriated profits or interest payments will be taxed at the US corporation tax level.

As a result, it can be stated that excess tax credits can be avoided by financing the investment with debt. Interest payments can be deducted and incur only withholding taxes, interest earnings in turn are taxed on the US parent level. Another possibility is to balance creditable taxes over several subsidiaries.

US parent companies also use other strategies to optimize their worldwide EATR. As a principal approach the repatriation of low taxed profits back to the US is generally deferred to the extent possible from a treasury point of view in order to avoid additional US cash taxes ("deferral structure"). In order to minimise excess tax credit positions, US groups try to manage their available tax credits by "mixing" high tax and low tax profits in such a way that the blended available tax credits match with the applicable limitation ("high–low planning"). Another strategy is to maximise the foreign tax credit limitation by maximizing the amount of foreign source income (higher foreign source profits or lower foreign source expenses). As the foreign tax credit limitation is defined by the ratio of foreign source income over worldwide taxable income multiplied by the US tax liability an increase of the foreign source income item has a positive impact on the applicable foreign tax credit limitation.

All tax planning strategies have to be reviewed under consideration of the US CFC rules (such as the attribution of subpart F income at the subsidiary level to the US parent without actual distributions).

5.3 Conclusion

The tax planning strategies show that there is a great potential for tax savings with regard to investments in the territories under review. For German multinationals, the main goal is to use the tax exemption of dividends to reduce the overall tax burden. For the United States in turn, the main objective must be to decrease excess tax credits.

But it has to be recognised that not only tax policies play a role in choosing the location of an investment. As the Asia-Pacific region includes highly developed as well as developing territories, other factors have to be taken into account, for example foreign exchange controls or political and legal security and stability. Of the territories selected, China, India, Indonesia, Japan, the Philippines, Taiwan, Thailand, and Vietnam impose laws on the control of foreign currency exchanges which certainly differ in their extent, but are, however, a disadvantage for foreign investors. A study done by Transparency International[5] examined the perceived corruption in Asian territories. Singapore, Australia, Hong Kong, Japan, Taiwan, South Korea, Malaysia are among the top third territories, with the least perceived corruption. In contrast Russia, Vietnam, Indonesia, the Philippines, and Cambodia are among the bottom third, representing a high level of perceived corruption. Certainly, the TI study has to be treated with care, although it still gives an insight to political stability.

[5]See Transparency International (2008).

Chapter 6
Corporate Taxation and Foreign Direct Investment Flows

6.1 Introduction: Corporate Taxation and International Investment Flows

The analysis in the preceding sections has focused on describing the tax burden faced by different types of foreign investment in the Asia-Pacific Region. In this section, we discuss the interaction between corporate tax burdens and actual foreign direct investment flows. In recent decades, governments across the world have become increasingly concerned about the impact of taxes on international investment flows. High tax countries fear that the tax burden on corporate investment may lead to a relocation of economic activity to countries with lower taxes. Some countries have actively pursued a low tax strategy with the objective to attract investment from other countries. In Europe, the significant decline in corporate income tax rates which occurred during the last two decades is widely seen as reflecting the forces of corporate tax competition. In East Asia, governments are at least as concerned about attracting foreign direct investment as governments in other regions.

The location of foreign direct investment depends on a large number of factors. Next to taxes, these include the proximity to clients or suppliers, the availability of key inputs like qualified employees or financial services, regulations, political stability of a country and many more. But the particular importance of taxes is due to the fact that taxes can be changed relatively easily and quickly whereas other important factors like e.g. proximity to markets or the availability of qualified employees can either not be changed at all or only in the long term.

In this section, we raise two related questions: Firstly, do we observe a process towards corporate income tax cuts as one would expect if territories compete for foreign direct investment? Secondly, is there a significant impact of taxes or tax incentives on foreign direct investment flows and if so, how large is this impact? Mainly for reasons of comparability and data availability, we focus on the following

D. Endres et al. (eds.), *Company Taxation in the Asia-Pacific Region, India, and Russia*,
DOI 10.1007/978-3-642-12217-0_6, © Springer-Verlag Berlin Heidelberg 2010

group of ten East Asian territories: China, India, Indonesia, Hong Kong, South Korea, Malaysia, the Philippines, Singapore, Thailand, Taiwan.[1]

The rest of the chapter is structured as follows. In Sections 6.2 and 6.3, we briefly discuss the development of tax policy in East Asia over time. Since many detailed features of the current tax systems have been described in the preceding sections, we focus on the development of two key elements of the tax system, which are particularly important in the context of FDI location and tax competition: the tax rates and special investment incentives like e.g. tax holidays. Section 6.4 gives an overview of the development of FDI flows to East Asia. In Section 6.5, we investigate whether differences in tax rates and tax incentives across territories and sectors have had a significant impact on investment flows. Section 6.6 concludes.

6.2 The Development of Corporate Income Tax Rates Over Time

In this section we briefly discuss the development of corporate taxation in East Asia over time, in particular the last two decades. We focus on the headline corporate tax rates and the role of special tax incentives for investment. Consider first the development of corporate tax rates. Figure 6.1 compares the unweighted average of the corporate tax rates in our group of East Asian territories to the development of average corporate tax rate in the EU 15, for the period between 1991 and 2008.

For the development in East Asia, three periods can be distinguished. In the early 1990s, there is a downward trend as the average tax rate declines from

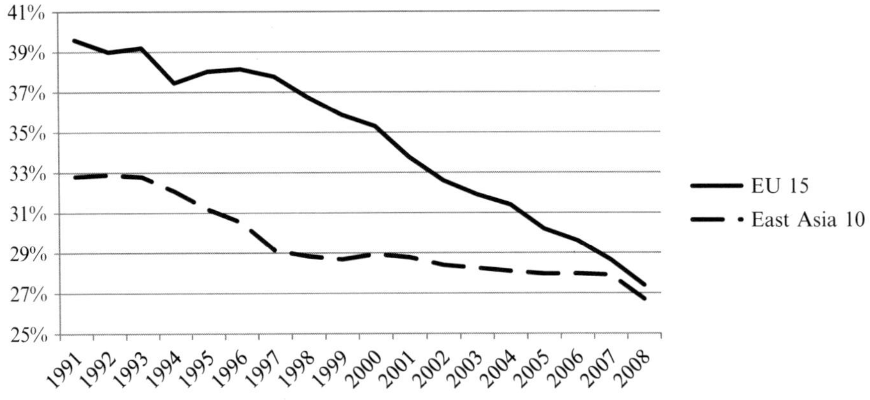

Fig. 6.1 Average corporate income tax rates in East Asia 10 and EU 15

[1]We exclude Japan and Australia because they are established OECD countries, where FDI flows are driven by rather different economic forces. Russia is a special case because of its geographical extension and Vietnam and Cambodia are excluded mainly because of limited data availability.

approximately 33% in 1991 to 29% in 1997. This is followed by a period of roughly 10 years where the average tax rate is almost stable. Finally, during the last 2 years, the average tax rate declines again, to 27% in 2008 and 26% in 2009. To some extent, this is driven by China, where the headline corporate tax rate was reduced from 33% in 2007 to 25% since 2008. Several other territories have also started reducing their tax rates. In comparison to this, the decline in corporate tax rates in Europe has been more steady and more pronounced. Between 1991 and 2008 the average corporate tax rate in the EU 15 has fallen from just under 40 to 27%.

The sharp fall in tax rates in Europe is widely seen as the result of intensive corporate tax competition within the EU. This downward pressure seems to have been slightly weaker in East Asia, but it should be taken into account that the initial levels of tax rates were already lower. Interestingly, the current levels of tax rates in the two regions are, on average, roughly similar. Of course, adding the new EU member states would change this picture – in 2008, the average corporate income tax rate in the EU 27 was equal to 23.5%.

The development of the average corporate tax rate in East Asia is the result of rather different trends in the individual territories. Roughly, two groups of territories can be distinguished. Figure 6.2 describes the development of the tax rates in a first group of territories which includes Hong Kong, China, Indonesia, the Philippines, Thailand, and Taiwan. In these territories, tax rates were at very different levels in 1991, with Hong Kong being the low tax territory. But all territories have held their tax rate levels more or less constant during the last two decades. Only very recently, since 2008, some of these territories, in particular China as mentioned above, have cut their rates.

The second group of territories includes Singapore, Malaysia, India and South Korea. These territories have steadily reduced their tax rates, as shown in Fig. 6.3. Among these territories, Singapore is the one with the lowest tax rate.

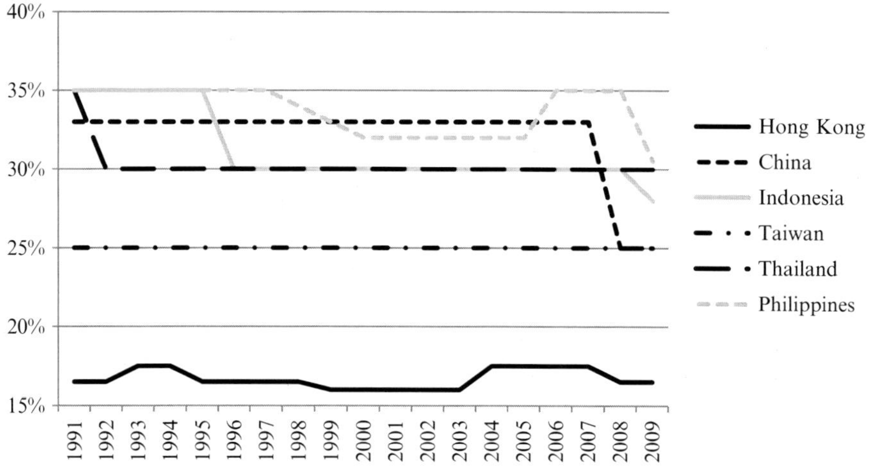

Fig. 6.2 Corporate tax rates in selected territories in East Asia

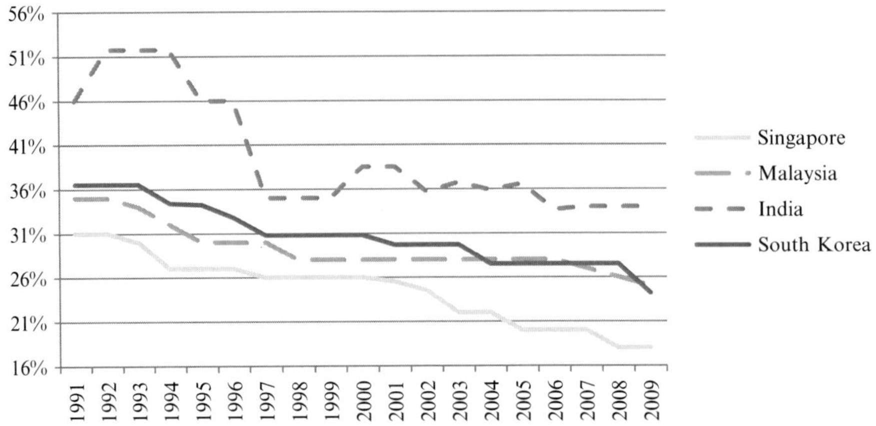

Fig. 6.3 Corporate tax rates in selected territories in East Asia

In general, the development of headline corporate income tax rates in East Asia suggests that these territories do follow the worldwide trend towards lower corporate tax rates, albeit not as radically as many European countries.

6.3 The Role of Tax Incentives

In East Asia, special tax incentives for investment play an important role. As has been shown in Chap. 4 of this report, all territories in East Asia considered here currently use various forms of investment incentives. These include tax holidays, exemptions from various taxes and tariffs, special economic zones, special investment depreciation provisions or investment tax credits, reduced tax rates and other forms of support. Chapter 4 of this report has demonstrated that these incentives can reduce the effective tax burden on inbound foreign direct investment considerably.

In the literature on the economic effects of special investment incentives, the evaluation of these incentives as a policy instrument is controversial. While it is recognized that investment incentives may allow countries to attract foreign direct investment, many economists are sceptical that the benefits of these incentives outweigh the costs. The costs of incentives are not limited to the tax revenue losses. Investment incentives also make the tax system more complex and difficult to administer, they may induce distortions between firms, sectors, and regions, and they may lead to more rent seeking or even fraud and corruption. Investment incentives are sometimes also seen as an instrument of harmful tax competition (see, e.g. Klemm (2009)). However, some authors have also pointed to positive aspects of investment incentives. For instance, Keen (2001) points out that differentiation in the taxation of bases with different degrees of mobility may reduce the intensity of tax competition and increase tax revenue, compared to a situation where no such differentiation is possible. From this perspective, special investment incentives allow countries to limit tax reductions to highly mobile investment, rather than total investment. Of course, the empirical relevance of this argument is an open question.

Our analysis focuses on the question of whether tax incentives have a significant impact on investment flows, not on the efficiency of these instruments from the perspective of the economy as a whole. In order to investigate whether incentives have affected foreign direct investment flows in East Asia, we need information on the development of tax incentives in the past. Since many investment incentives focus on specific industries or sectors, our empirical analysis exploits the fact that different territories in East Asia have put emphasis on different industries. We then analyse the sectoral composition of FDI flows and ask whether these flows are affected by the presence of targeted incentives. We consider the period 2002–2007 because data for foreign direct investment flows at the sectoral level is only available for the time after 2002. In the empirical analysis, we simply distinguish between territories which have special incentives in a certain sector and territories which do not. Table 6.1 gives an overview of the investment incentives in the different territories. Since no territory either newly introduced or completely abolished special sectoral incentives in this time span, the information in Table 6.1 applies to the entire period.

6.4 Foreign Direct Investment Flows

The dynamic economic development of many territories in East Asia during the last decades has been reflected in growing flows of foreign direct investment to these territories. Figure 6.4 illustrates that overall inward foreign direct investment flows, measured in US-Dollars, have grown between 1980 and 2007 by a factor of roughly 60.

Figure 6.4 also shows that foreign direct investment flows have been growing rather steadily until the Asian Economic Crisis in the mid-1990s. After a short decline during this crisis, FDI flows have started growing even more quickly, only briefly interrupted in the years 2001–2003. Since FDI includes mergers and acquisitions, it is likely that the peak in 2000 and the subsequent decline can partly be explained by the wave of mergers and acquisitions in this period. The impact of the recent global economic crisis is not included in these figures because FDI statistics are not yet available. How do these FDI flows compare to global FDI? Figure 6.5 illustrates the development of global FDI inflows, also measured in US-Dollars. Clearly, the dynamic growth of FDI is a global phenomenon. In 2007, global FDI flows were roughly 34 times higher than in 1980.

Table 6.1 Sectoral investment incentives in East Asia

	China	India	Indonesia	Malaysia	Korea	Philippines	Singapore	Taiwan	Hong Kong	Thailand
Not allocated and agric.	0	0	0	1	1	1	0	0	0	1
Mining and quarrying	0	0	1	0	1	1	0	0	0	1
Total petroleum, chemical, rubber, plastic products	1	1	1	1	1	1	0	1	0	1
Non-allocated manufacturing/other manufacturing	1	1	1	1	1	0	0	0	0	1
Total office machinery, computers, RTV, communication equipments	1	1	1	1	1	1	0	1	0	1
Total vehicles and other transport equipment	1	1	1	1	1	1	0	1	0	1
Electricity, gas and water	1	1	0	0	1	1	0	0	0	1
Construction	1	1	0	0	1	0	0	0	0	1
Trade and repairs	1	0	0	0	1	0	0	0	0	1
Hotels and restaurants	1	0	0	1	1	1	0	0	0	1
Transport, storage and communication	1	0	0	1	1	0	1	0	0	1
Financial intermediation	1	0	0	1	1	0	1	0	1	0
Computer activities	1	1	1	1	1	1	1	0	0	1
Research and development	1	0	0	1	1	1	1	1	0	1
Other business activities	1	1	0	1	1	1	1	0	1	1
Recreational, cultural and sporting activities	1	0	0	1	1	0	1	0	0	1
Other services	1	0	0	0	1	0	0	0	0	1

1 there is a special investment incentive for this sector, *0* there is no special investment incentive for this sector

Source: PwC and various other sources

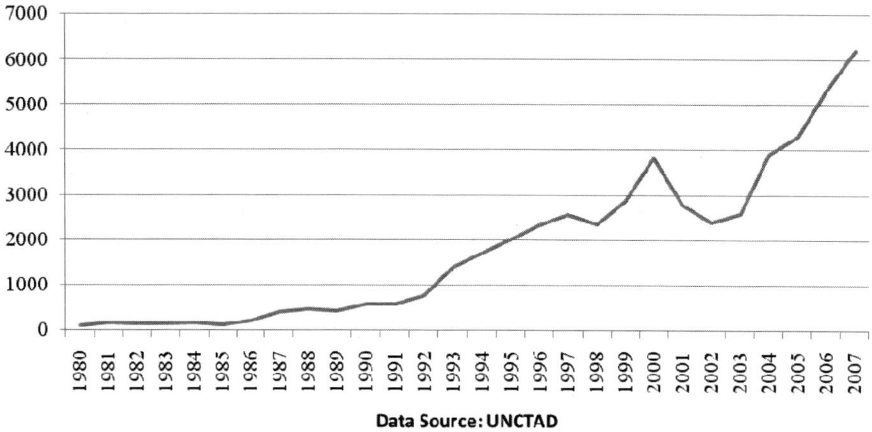

Fig. 6.4 Foreign direct investment in East Asia 10 (1980 = 100)

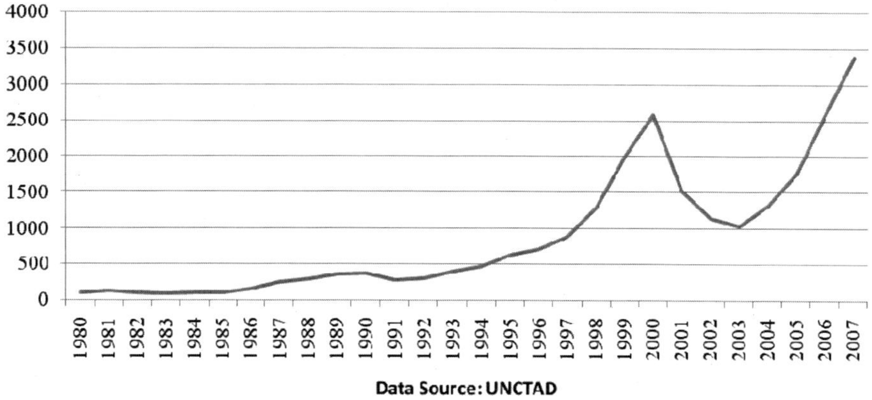

Fig. 6.5 Worldwide foreign direct investment flows (1980 = 100)

In addition, Fig. 6.5 shows that the volatility in global FDI flows, in particular the boom at the end of the 1990s, was more pronounced than in East Asia. A possible explanation would be that mergers and acquisitions, which are strongly correlated to the development of stock markets, are less important for FDI in East Asia, compared to the global average. Figure 6.6 depicts the share of our group of East Asian territories in global FDI.

Overall, the share of East Asia in global FDI has increased between 1980 and 2007. This reflects that their nominal volume has grown more quickly than the volume of global FDI, as mentioned above. But the increase in the FDI share is perhaps less than one would expect. It has grown from 7% in 1980 to approximately 12.5% in 2007. Interestingly, during the same period, the share of these territories in worldwide GDP has grown by a similar magnitude, from just under 6% to

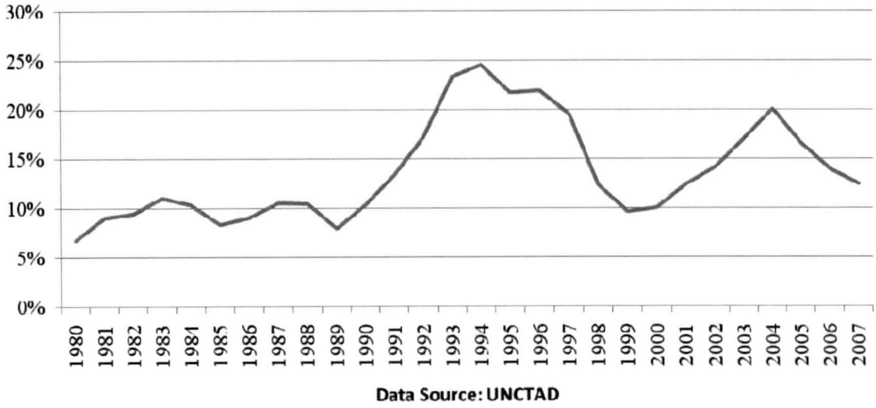

Fig. 6.6 Share of East Asia 10 in worldwide FDI inflows

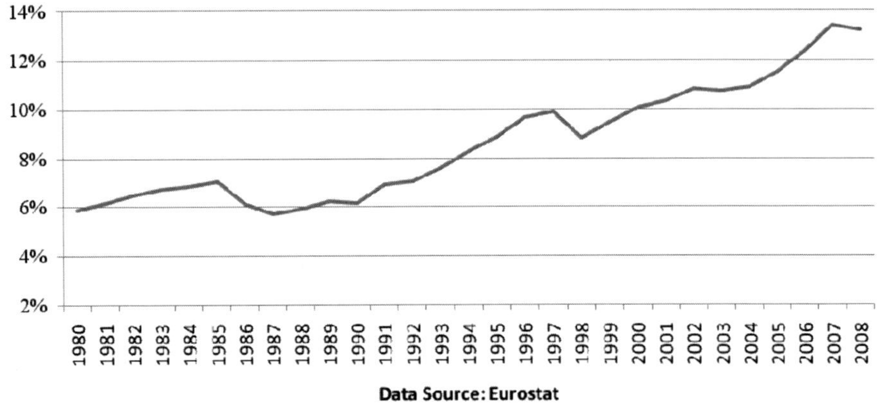

Fig. 6.7 Share of East Asia 10 in World GDP

approximately 13%. Of course, the growth in the GDP share has been much less volatile, as illustrated by Fig. 6.7.

Another striking feature of the share of East Asia in global FDI flows is that this share is rather volatile. This volatility is mostly driven by the volatility of FDI flows in the rest of the world. As mentioned above, a possible explanation would be that mergers and acquisitions, which are highly volatile, play a smaller role in FDI flows to the group of East Asian territories under consideration than in flows between Europe, North America, and Japan.

How are FDI flows to East Asia distributed across territories? Figure 6.8 shows the distribution of FDI flows across territories in 1980. At this point in time, roughly three quarters of all FDI went to three territories: Hong Kong, Singapore and Malaysia. Clearly, in 1980, economic reforms in China had only just begun, and the country played a negligible role as a location for foreign direct investment.

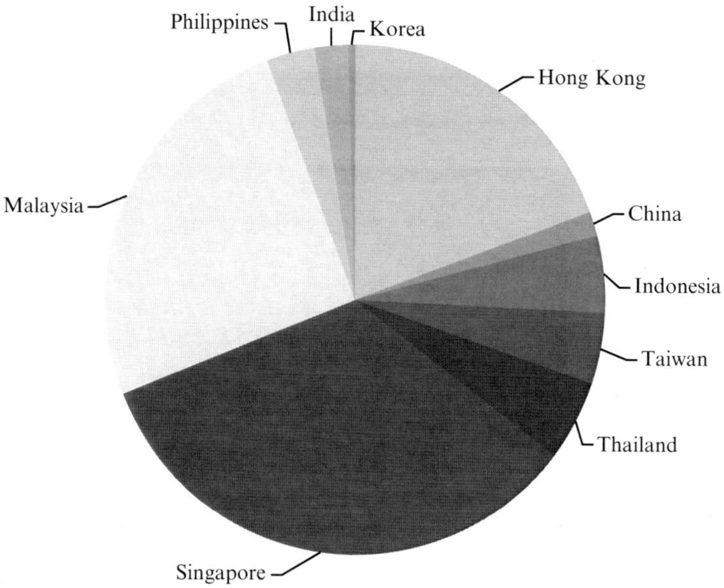

Fig. 6.8 Structure of FDI flows to East Asia in 1980
Source: UNCTAD

In the following three decades, the situation changed fundamentally. This is illustrated by Fig. 6.9. In 2007 China attracted approximately one third of the FDI flows going to this region. Hong Kong was the second largest importer of foreign direct investment. To a large extent, this reflects that Hong Kong is a location for many holding companies, on particular companies with operations in China, and the most important financial centre in the region. Singapore is still an important location for FDI but its share has diminished compared to 1980, as has the share of Malaysia.

6.5 Do Taxes and Investment Incentives Drive Foreign Direct Investment Flows to East Asia?

In our sample of Asian territories, corporate income tax rates have a negative effect on foreign direct investment. The correlation between FDI and tax rates is −0.19. Of course, there are large differences in territory size in our sample, so it is more sensible to look at relative changes in FDI. The relevant correlation between the logarithm of FDI and tax rates is even stronger with a value of −0.45. In order to be sure that the negative relationship between FDI and taxes is not just coincidental, we control for other factors by means of a regression. In this way, we take into account time trends, differences in economic growth and other inherent differences between territories. Nevertheless, the negative effect of corporate income taxes on FDI persists. The results, which are displayed in Table 6.2, indicate that lowering the corporate income tax rate by 1% point increases FDI by 5%. Further results are,

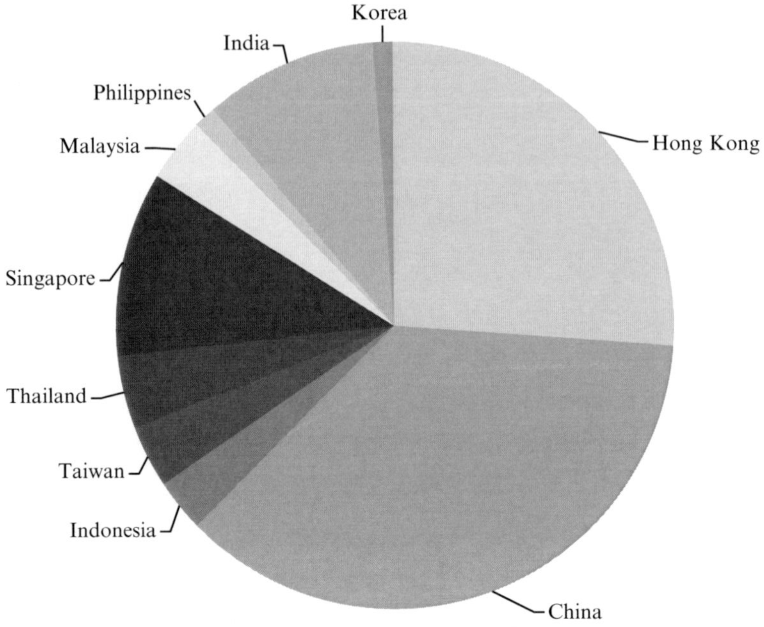

Fig. 6.9 Structure of FDI flows to East Asia in 2007
Source: UNCTAD

Table 6.2 Regression results overall FDI flows

Variables	
Corporate income tax rate	−5.008** (2.092)
Log (GDP)	−4.787*** (1.669)
Log (GDP per capita)	5.213*** (1.376)
Log (government consumption)	0.0635 (0.730)
Openness	−0.127 (0.219)
Inflation rate	−0.0282** (0.0129)
Observations	196
R-squared	0.866

Standard errors in *parentheses*
***$p < 0.01$, **$p < 0.05$, *$p < 0.1$

firstly, that an inflationary environment deters FDI. An increase in inflation by 1% point lowers FDI by 2.8%. Secondly, increasing wealth levels – represented by GDP per capita – attract FDI. Of course, a growing GDP per capita may also represent increasing skills in the labor force. On the other hand, simply growing in absolute size – and not in per capita terms – for example due to strong population growth – has a negative effect on FDI.[2]

As mentioned before, statutory tax rates are only one aspect of a country's tax system. Especially in Asian territories there are numerous incentives for investment

[2] A 1% increase in GDP (with constant GDP per capita) lowers FDI by 4.8%.

in form of special deductions or tax vacations for certain activities (as opposed to European countries where the rules of the common market hamper preferential tax treatment).[3] Literally all territories under consideration have had these special incentives. An exception which proves the rule is Indonesia which tried to continue without special incentives for some years but re-introduced them in the late 90s.

An analysis of special incentive programs' effect on FDI is possible with European data on FDI in Asia that distinguishes between different sectors. Figures 6.10 and 6.11 illustrate how the sectoral allocation of FDI across Asian territories differs from the sectoral allocation of total FDI. On the one hand, FDI in *Manufacturing* accounts for 34% (versus 19% in total FDI). On the other hand, the share of FDI in *Financial Intermediation*, *Other Business Activities*, and *Transport, Storage and Communication* is significantly smaller than usual.

In order to identify the effect of special incentive programs on FDI, we exploit differences in the structure of incentive programs across territories. For a certain sector, some territories offer tax incentives, others do not. Does the former group of

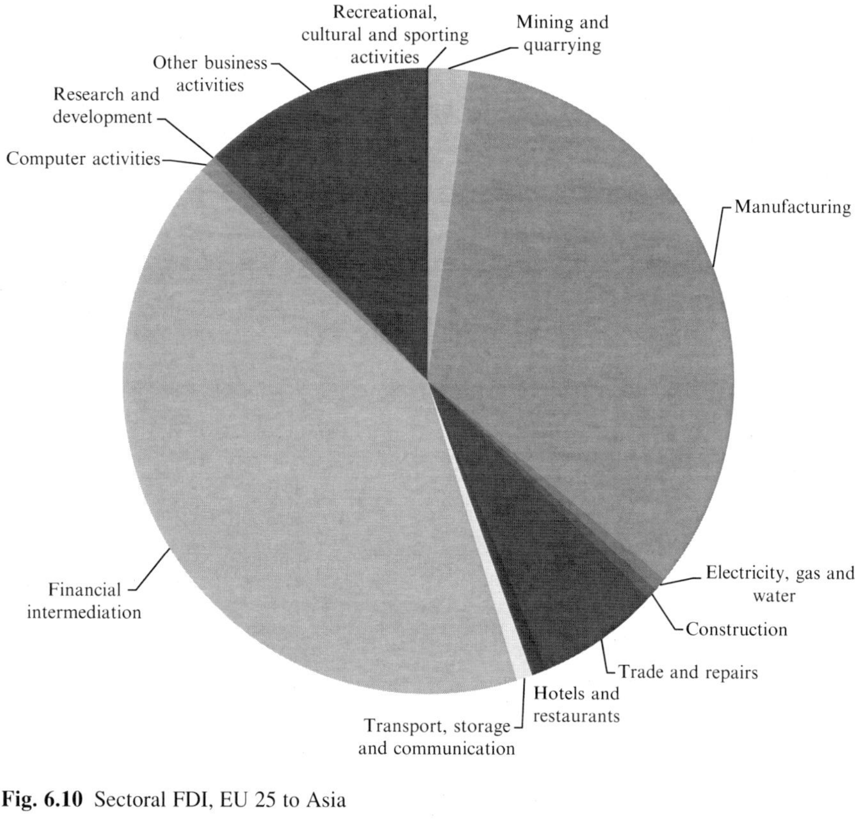

Fig. 6.10 Sectoral FDI, EU 25 to Asia

[3]For example, the Netherlands had to abolish preferential treatment for logistics centres. The Channel Islands had to abandon the practice of ring-fencing their off-shore financial industry.

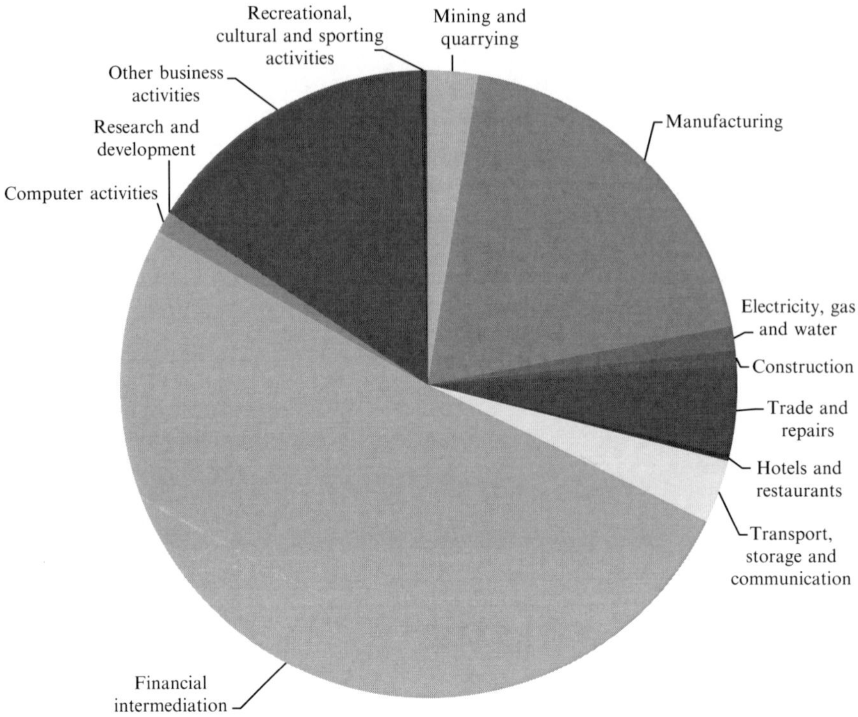

Fig. 6.11 Sectoral FDI, EU 25 to World

territories receive relatively more FDI in that sector than the latter group?[4] The correlation between FDI in a certain sector and the presence of special tax incentives for that sector is 0.04. As before, the size of FDI flows differs strongly with the size of the destination country, the country of origin and across sectors. Hence, the more relevant measure is the logarithm of FDI flows which captures relative changes in FDI. The correlation with respect to the presence of tax incentives is 0.13. By means of regression analysis we control for other potential factors that influence FDI flows to certain sectors. The same control variables as in the previous analysis are employed. Furthermore, we account for inherent differences between different time periods, sectors, source countries, and destination countries.

The regression results in Table 6.3 imply that FDI in sectors with special tax incentives is 28% larger than without special incentives. This result underlines the importance of tax features besides statutory rates for investment decisions.[5]

[4]Although all countries constantly announce reforms of their special incentive programs, the eventual adjustments are very marginal for the period from 2002 to 2007, for which FDI data across sectors is available. Hence differences over time cannot be exploited to identify the effect of incentive programs.

[5]The result is based on cross-sectional variance. Hence, the argument can justifiably be turned around. Countries may install special tax incentives for sectors in which they are already attractive for foreign investors. This could imply that foreign investors are able to lobby for their advantage.

Table 6.3 Regression results sectoral FDI flows

Variables	(1)
Special tax incentive	0.285** (0.137)
Corporate income tax rate	−9.726 (6.656)
Log (GDP)	−4.238 (7.121)
Log (GDP per capita)	8.030 (6.704)
Log (government consumption)	0.129 (1.801)
Openness	−0.277 (0.552)
Inflation rate	−0.0217
Observations	3,213

Standard errors in *parentheses*
***$p < 0.01$, **$p < 0.05$, *$p < 0.1$

The other control variables are similar to the previous regression in Table 6.2. In particular, high tax rates seem to affect FDI negatively. The insignificance of the control variables is not surprising: they do not vary across sectors and the period of observation from 2002 to 2007 is too short for sufficient variation over time. A longer sample is warranted for more significant control variables.

6.6 Conclusion

The analysis in this chapter has focused on the interaction between corporate taxation including special investment incentives and foreign direct investment flows to East Asia. In the period between 1990 and 2007, corporate income tax rates in east Asia have declined significantly on average, albeit not as much as in the EU. At the same time, all territories under consideration have used various special investment incentives. Our analysis has shown that flows of foreign direct investment to East Asia are affected by differences in the corporate tax burden and, in particular, special investment incentives. The results indicate that lowering the corporate income tax rate by 1% point increases FDI by 5%. Our results for the impact of special investment incentives imply that FDI in sectors with special tax incentives is 28% larger than without special incentives. This result underlines the importance of tax features besides statutory rates for investment decisions. One should take into account, however, that these results may also have a different interpretation: The presence of FDI in a sector increases the likelihood that special investment incentives are introduced.

Appendix

Table A.1 Exchange rates as of 10 November 2009

Currency	1 EUR =
Australian Dollar	1.6132
Cambodia Riel	6,256.1798
Chinese Yuan	10.2330
Hong Kong Dollar	11.6106
Indian Rupee	69.7528
Indonesian Rupiah	14,157.3034
Japanese Yen	134.5993
Malaysian Ringgit	5.0659
Philippine Peso	70.2547
Russian Rouble	43.0286
Singapore Dollar	2.7093
Korean Won	1,730.0375
Taiwan Dollar	48.6592
Thai Baht	49.8951
US Dollar	1.4981

Table A.2 Effective average tax rates at subsidiary level

Territory	Overall average (%)	Average for each source of finance			Average for each asset				
		Retained earnings (%)	New equity (%)	Debt (%)	Buildings (%)	Intangibles (%)	Machinery (%)	Financial assets (%)	Inventories (%)
Australia	28.3	31.9	31.9	21.5	25.4	33.3	25.6	29.3	27.8
Cambodia	18.3	20.8	20.8	13.8	16.4	18.7	18.5	19.5	18.5
China	23.9	26.9	26.9	18.2	24.3	23.4	24.2	24.4	23.2
Hong Kong	10.3	11.9	11.9	7.3	13.0	11.5	11.6	0.0	15.3
India	40.0	42.9	48.8	33.0	42.9	37.4	39.4	40.9	39.5
Indonesia	26.8	30.2	30.2	20.4	23.7	27.9	29.0	27.3	26.0
Japan	42.1	47.0	47.0	32.8	41.7	40.6	39.7	44.1	44.1
Malaysia	22.3	25.4	25.4	16.7	21.2	20.3	22.5	24.4	23.2
Philippines	31.9	35.6	35.6	25.0	37.5	26.4	37.9	29.3	28.4
Russia	21.7	24.1	24.1	17.1	26.3	18.7	26.3	19.5	17.6

(*continued*)

Table A.2 (continued)

Territory	Overall average (%)	Average for each source of finance			Average for each asset				
		Retained earnings (%)	New equity (%)	Debt (%)	Buildings (%)	Intangibles (%)	Machinery (%)	Financial assets (%)	Inventories (%)
Singapore	15.9	18.1	18.1	11.8	16.5	14.6	13.9	17.6	16.7
South Korea	22.5	25.4	25.4	17.0	26.0	22.6	18.9	23.6	21.3
Taiwan	22.1	26.5	22.6	15.1	28.8	25.0	23.4	10.3	23.0
Thailand	26.9	30.5	30.5	20.1	27.9	25.9	24.9	29.3	26.3
Vietnam	22.7	25.8	25.8	17.1	21.7	23.4	22.3	24.4	22.0
Germany	28.1	31.4	31.4	21.9	28.9	25.5	27.9	30.5	27.5
USA	37.4	42.1	42.1	28.6	38.0	40.1	36.9	37.9	34.1

Table A.3 Effective average tax rates on German outbound investments to the Asia-Pacific region (parent company level)

Territory	Overall average (%)	Subsidiary source of finance		
		Retained earnings (%)	New equity (%)	Debt (%)
Australia	38.3	35.8	41.5	37.8
Cambodia	29.3	25.9	31.3	30.7
China	31.5	29.2	33.2	32.2
Hong Kong	11.8	9.6	10.1	15.8
India	42.5	40.1	46.4	41.1
Indonesia	34.1	32.1	36.1	34.2
Japan	47.7	46.9	51.0	45.2
Malaysia	23.7	22.8	23.4	25.0
Philippines	38.7	36.8	40.9	38.3
Russia	26.3	24.1	26.4	28.4
Singapore	17.3	15.6	16.2	20.2
South Korea	27.1	25.4	27.6	28.2
Taiwan	37.9	35.4	41.0	37.4
Thailand	34.2	32.4	36.4	33.8
Vietnam	24.1	23.2	23.8	25.4

Table A.4 Effective average tax rates on US outbound investments to the Asia-Pacific region (parent company level)

Territory	Overall average (%)	Subsidiary source of finance		
		Retained earnings (%)	New equity (%)	Debt (%)
Australia	31.9	30.3	32.8	32.8
Cambodia	30.6	26.2	32.7	32.7
China	31.7	28.6	33.2	33.2
Hong Kong	28.8	23.1	31.7	31.7
India	40.9	38.1	44.1	40.5
Indonesia	32.2	29.9	33.4	33.4
Japan	41.6	42.3	42.3	40.3
Malaysia	30.3	27.2	31.9	31.9
Philippines	39.6	36.7	42.0	40.1
Russia	33.3	28.9	35.5	35.5
Singapore	29.9	25.1	32.3	32.3
South Korea	31.1	27.8	32.7	32.7
Taiwan	37.0	34.0	39.5	37.4
Thailand	32.3	30.2	33.7	33.0
Vietnam	30.7	27.6	32.2	32.2

Table A.5 Effective average tax rates in the Asia-Pacific region (subsidiary level) considering tax incentives for the year 2009

Territory	Overall average (%)	Average for each source of finance			Average for each asset				
		Retained earnings (%)	New equity (%)	Debt (%)	Buildings (%)	Intangibles (%)	Machinery (%)	Financial assets (%)	Inventories (%)
Australia	28.28	31.93	31.93	21.49	25.38	33.33	25.56	29.29	27.82
Cambodia	12.14	13.75	13.75	9.14	10.87	12.38	12.23	12.93	12.29
China	11.72	13.17	13.17	9.04	13.50	11.08	11.47	11.58	11.00
Hong Kong	10.27	11.88	11.88	7.29	12.99	11.48	11.60	0.00	15.30
India	22.37	24.17	26.72	18.30	27.06	20.08	21.24	22.15	21.32
Indonesia	23.39	26.81	26.81	17.06	21.03	21.14	21.51	27.33	25.96
Japan	42.05	47.03	47.03	32.81	41.71	40.58	39.73	44.13	44.13
Malaysia	11.24	12.77	12.77	8.39	10.65	10.24	11.32	12.29	11.67
Philippines	23.04	25.48	25.48	18.50	29.33	17.73	29.65	19.41	19.07
Russia	19.60	22.05	22.05	15.06	22.21	16.27	22.45	19.52	17.56
Singapore	5.94	6.73	6.73	4.49	7.28	5.23	4.96	6.28	5.96
South Korea	15.28	17.25	17.25	11.62	18.73	15.09	12.62	15.77	14.18
Taiwan	22.10	26.48	22.61	15.05	28.78	25.02	23.42	10.26	22.99
Thailand	13.76	15.59	15.59	10.36	15.63	12.92	12.46	14.63	13.16
Vietnam	10.19	11.56	11.56	7.66	9.72	10.47	9.98	10.94	9.85

Table A.6 Effective average tax rates on German outbound investments to the Asia-Pacific region (parent company level) considering tax incentives for the year 2009

Territory	Overall average (%)	Subsidiary source of finance		
		Retained earnings (%)	New equity (%)	Debt (%)
Australia	38.35	35.76	41.51	37.76
Cambodia	13.64	11.40	11.94	17.58
China	20.71	17.01	21.03	24.09
Hong Kong	11.80	9.56	10.09	15.75
India	24.32	21.64	24.70	26.62
Indonesia	31.11	29.07	33.09	31.17
Japan	47.70	46.93	50.98	45.17
Malaysia	12.75	10.43	10.97	16.84
Philippines	30.77	27.87	31.92	32.51
Russia	24.38	22.20	24.49	26.44
Singapore	7.50	4.48	5.02	13.01
South Korea	19.13	16.76	18.47	22.15
Taiwan	37.91	35.40	40.98	37.37
Thailand	18.88	16.17	18.45	22.03
Vietnam	11.71	9.24	9.78	16.12

Table A.7 Effective average tax rates on US outbound investments to the Asia-Pacific region (parent company level) considering tax incentives for the year 2009

Territory	Overall average (%)	Subsidiary source of finance		
		Retained earnings (%)	New equity (%)	Debt (%)
Australia	31.93	30.28	32.76	32.76
Cambodia	30.20	24.38	33.11	33.11
China	30.77	24.67	33.82	33.82
Hong Kong	28.80	23.06	31.67	31.67
India	31.51	26.71	33.90	33.90
Indonesia	29.19	26.89	30.38	30.31
Japan	41.61	42.26	42.26	40.33
Malaysia	29.94	23.99	32.92	32.92
Philippines	34.16	29.81	36.27	36.41
Russia	31.60	27.23	33.79	33.79
Singapore	29.93	22.84	33.47	33.47
South Korea	30.72	25.49	33.33	33.33
Taiwan	36.98	34.04	39.53	37.38
Thailand	30.31	24.84	33.04	33.04
Vietnam	30.04	23.83	33.15	33.15

Table A.8 Withholding tax rates on dividends in the Asia-Pacific region, India, and Russia (%)

	Australia	Cambodia	China	Germany	Hong Kong	India	Indonesia	Japan	Malaysia	Philippines	Russia	Singapore	South Korea	Taiwan	Thailand	USA	Vietnam
Australia	–	30	15	15	30	15	15	5	15	15	5	15	15	15	20	0	15
Cambodia	14	–	14	14	14	14	14	14	14	14	14	14	14	14	14	14	14
China	10	10	–	10	5	10	10	10	10	10	10	5	5	10	10	10	10
Hong Kong	0	0	0	0	–	0	0	0	0	0	0	0	0	0	0	0	0
India	0	0	0	0	0	–	0	0	0	0	0	0	0	0	0	0	0
Indonesia	15	20	10	10	20	10	–	10	10	15	15	10	10	10	15	10	15
Japan	15	20	10	10	20	10	10	–	5	10	20	5	5	20	15	0	10
Malaysia	0	0	0	0	0	0	0	0	–	0	0	0	0	0	0	0	0
Philippines	15	15	10	10	15	15	15	10	15	–	15	15	10	15	15	15	10
Russia	5	15	10	5	15	10	15	15	15	15	–	15	5	15	15	5	10
Singapore	0	0	0	0	0	0	0	0	0	0	0	–	0	0	0	0	0
South Korea	15	27.5	5	5	27.5	15	10	5	10	11	5	10	–	27.5	15	11	10
Taiwan	10	25	25	20	25	25	10	25	12.5	25	25	[a]	25	–	25	25	15
Thailand	10	10	10	10	10	10	10	10	10	10	10	10	10	10	–	10	10
Vietnam	0	0	0	0	0	0	0	0	0	0	0	0	0	0	0	0	–

[a]Underlying corporate tax and withholding tax may not exceed 40%

Table A.9 Withholding tax rates on interest in the Asia-Pacific region, India, and Russia (%)

	Australia	Cambodia	China	Germany	Hong Kong	India	Indonesia	Japan	Malaysia	Philippines	Russia	Singapore	South Korea	Taiwan	Thailand	USA	Vietnam
Australia	–	10	10	10	10	10	10	10	15	15	10	10	15	10	10	10	10
Cambodia	14	–	14	14	14	14	14	14	14	14	14	14	14	14	14	14	14
China	10	10	–	10	7	10	10	10	10	10	10	10	10	10	10	10	10
Hong Kong	0	0	0	0	–	0	0	0	0	0	0	0	0	0	0	0	0
India	15	20	10	10	20	–	10	10	10	15	10	15	15	20	20	15	10
Indonesia	15	20	10	10	20	10	–	10	10	10	15	10	10	10	15	10	15
Japan	10	15	10	10	15	10	10	–	10	10	15	10	10	15	15	10	10
Malaysia	15	15	10	15	15	10	15	10	–	15	15	10	15	10	15	15	10
Philippines	15	30	10	15	30	15	15	15	15	–	15	15	15	30	15	15	15
Russia	10	20	10	0	20	10	15	10	15	15	–	20	0	20	20	0	10
Singapore	10	15	10	8	15	15	10	10	10	15	15	–	0	15	15	15	10
South Korea	15	27.5	10	10	27.5	15	10	10	15	16.5	27.5	10	–	27.5	10	13.2	10
Taiwan	10	20	20	20	20	20	10	20	10	20	20	20	20	–	20	20	10
Thailand	15	15	15	15	15	15	15	15	15	15	15	15	15	15	–	15	15
Vietnam	10	10	10	10	10	10	10	10	10	15	10	10	10	10	10	10	–

References

IBFD (2009) Asia-Pacific – Taxation & Investment Database, Online

Census and Statistics Department (2008) 2008 Annual survey of companies in Hong Kong representing parent companies located outside Hong Kong. Census and Statistics Department, Hong Kong

de Mooij RA, Ederveen S (2003) Taxation and foreign direct investment: a synthesis of empirical research. Int Tax Public Finance 10:673–693

Deutsche Bundesbank (1989–2007) Bestandserhebung über Direktinvestitionen, http://www.bundesbank.de/statistik/statistik_zeitreihen.php?open=aussenwirtschaft

Devereux MP, Griffith R (1999) The taxation of discrete investment choices – revision 2. In: IFS Working Paper Series No. W98/16, London

Devereux MP, Elschner C, Endres D, Heckemeyer JH, Overesch M, Schreiber U, Spengel C (2008) Effective levels of company taxation within an enlarged EU, Project for the EU Commission TAXUD 2005/DE/3 10, Final Report, EU Commission, Mannheim

Bureau of Economic Analyses (1989–2007) US Direct Investment Abroad, http://www.bea.gov/international/di1usdbal.htm

European Commission (2001) Company taxation in the internal market, SEC(2001) 1681, Luxembourg

Hunya G (2006) How to assess the impact of FDI on an economy? Vienna Institute for International Economic Studies, Vienna

Jacobs OH (2008) Internationale Unternehmensbesteuerung, Munich

Katz J (2002) Get me headquarters. Region Rev 12:9–19

Keen M (2001) Preferential regimes can make tax competition less harmful. Natl Tax J 54:757–762

Klemm A (2009) Causes, benefits, and risks of business tax incentives. In: IMF Working Paper No. 09/21

PricewaterhouseCoopers (2008) Worldwide tax summaries

Schreiber U, Spengel C, Lammersen L (2002) Measuring the impact of taxation on investment and financing decisions. Schmalenbachs Bus Rev 54:2–23

Testa W, Klier T, Ono Y (2005) The changing relationship between headquarters and cities. Chicago Fed Letter No. 212a, The Federal Reserve Bank of Chicago

Transparency International (2008) Corruption Perception Index, http://www.transparency.org/policy_research/surveys_indices/cpi/2008

UNCTAD (2009) World investment report 2009. UNCTAD, New York, NY

Printed by Books on Demand, Germany